GW00391191

From
a Faraway
Country

Peter Tegel

THE CONRAD PRESS

Published in the
United Kingdom by The Conrad Press

ISBN-10 1484031075
ISBN-13 978-1-48403-107-0

A CIP catalogue record
for this book is available
from the British Library.

Pre-press production
www.ebookversions.com

About the author

Peter Tegel, playwright and translator from Russian, German and French, has written numerous radio plays broadcast by BBC Radio 3, BBC Radio 4 and abroad – some dealing with material further developed in his memoir, such as *Return to Krnov* set in 1989, the year of the collapse of Communism, and *The So What Club* about a German refugee community in London immediately after the Second World War.

His other radio plays include an adaptation of his novel *Happy Depths of a Homophobe*, with Derek Jacobi (BBC Radio 3), which is also available in a Kindle ebook edition.

Peter Tegel's play translations have been performed by the Royal Shakespeare Company, the National and other theatres. His published play translations include Bertolt Brecht's *Baal* (Methuen) and Nicolai Erdman's *The Suicide* (Samuel French). For his translation of Uwe Timm's *The Snake Tree* (Picador) he shared the Schlegel Tieck prize.

Contents

From
a Faraway
Country

Peter Tegel

CHAPTER ONE

Mother into fish

The wind determines where the leaves will fall. Sometimes they blow onto the roof and collect in the gutters, sometimes into the street. That winter a fierce north-easterly had piled them onto the drive. I'd always burned them in the incinerator, but now it was March. I still hadn't done it.

Perhaps today I would.

It should have kept me busy. Besides, the garden incinerator safely indulges my passion for fire, there's something magical about the way the smoke pours from its funnel. When there's no wind to tease it, it drifts lazily. Sometimes it blows in all directions, a noxious cloud that chokes.

Instead, that Sunday I drove to my mother's flat.

I was aware, as always, how clean the building was. The carpet on the stairs to her landing was spotless. The winter sun came in through the skylight. I hesitated a moment before letting myself in. The hall was dark. I stood a while before turning on a light. I wanted to know if it would be as it was in my dream. I had stood as now outside her door, then let myself into her flat, into the darkness, and been overwhelmed by an emotion, perhaps loneliness, when I realised that the flat was empty.

What will you do when I'm gone?

Mother, you *have* gone!

It's as if I hear her reply: I know, I know! But she looks doubtful, her eyes baffled. She repeats: All the same, what *will* you do when I'm gone?

After the funeral we'd come back to the flat, drunk champagne from her crystal glasses and eaten off her best porcelain. Somewhere in the room an antique had backfired probably in protest against the central heating. That was your mother, said Mrs McGonagle. We'd laughed as people do after a funeral, given the opportunity, and raised our glasses to drink a toast: to Hilda!

Mrs McGonagle had washed up after the party and left everything stacked under kitchen towels. I paused, as if the shapes under the towels were a mystery not to be too soon solved, then pulled one of the towels away: the Meissen plates!

I want everything to stay as it is was.

But then, my mother has only been dead five days.

We'd found the plates together, she and I, on our Saturday forays without my stepfather Otto in the antique shops in Kensington Church Street during the war when I was home from school. There had been bargains then. I'd learned the hallmarks and developed a sharp eye and my mother soon had a collection of rare and beautiful porcelain.

I couldn't really think what to do in the flat. Should I take the paintings home, or at least the one: *Satyr and Nymph*? The desk was the only piece of furniture I intended to keep. I pulled open the drawers. They were crammed. I laid out the contents on the floor. There were pills and ointments, and her gall stones, a rusty red, in a transparent plastic box. I found Christmas and birthday cards we had sent to her over the last ten or fifteen years, and Otto's certificate to practice law, *Universitas Carolina Pragensis,* 31 May 1929. There was a shoe box stuffed with two decades of bank statements, reminding me, as if I needed reminding, of the touchstone of our feelings for each other: money. Then there was the folder marked *Meine Reise,* my journey: a memento of her cruise on the Europa round South America a year after Otto's death.

I went to my mother's bedroom. By her make-up stands a photograph of her brother, my uncle Franz, in his Prague student days, doe-eyed and delicate, with a duelling scar on his cheek. What happened to him, she had asked me. She'd forgotten where he had died and when. I'd told her that according to the family chronicle kept by a Czech relative Franz had become mayor of Reichenberg, then *Landrat,* District Administrator of the Sudeten Territories during the German occupation. She had begun to cry and said: I can't believe Franz did anything bad. He was not a Nazi. Whatever he did, she had insisted, would have been under duress. She'd repeated again and again: Franz did nothing bad. He was not a Nazi.

Back in the living room I opened the folder: *Meine Reise.* Inside were maps and brochures, and postcards of penguins in the Bay of Ushuaia, of seals on ice floes, and of the *Europa* in the Straits of Magellan. There were menus for gala dinners; Sevruga caviar and blinis off Puerto Madryn, Alaska crab with truffles off Tierra del Fuego, lobster at Puerto Montt, Brunswick salad at sea, and so it went on off Valparaiso, off Arica, Callao, with sevruga caviar again for the *Auf Wiedersehen* dinner at Guayaquil. The *Europa* was a German ship. I'd had an argument with my mother after I'd given her an illustrated, much abridged copy of *Voyage of the Beagle* to take with her on the cruise. Who was I to boast of my education for which after all she had paid? What right did I have to ask her sly questions such as: Who was Darwin? And shake my head when she told me the answer: that Darwin had discovered South America? That had been one of our better arguments, bordering on humour and ending with her sheepish grin.

I unfolded a sheet of mock parchment: *Taufschein,* certificate of baptism. At the top, a representation of the earth floated in blue space. Below on either side were cherubs on clouds. One peered at the earth through a telescope, the other was measuring it with a theodolite. Scrolls led down to, on the left, a schooner in full sail before the wind, on the right, Neptune emergent from the Depths, trident in hand. Centre bottom, the name of the shipping company: Hapag-Lloyd AG. Centre page, it stated:

> *We, Neptune, Lord of all Oceans, Seas, Rivers,*
> *Ponds, Puddles, Ditches and Swamps*
> *do graciously certify*
> *that today 1st February 1978*
> *on board the MS Europa*
> *Hilda Langer*
> *in crossing the Line was cleansed*
> *of the filth of the Northern Hemisphere*
> *and after due medical examination*
> *baptised with the greenish-blue waters of the wake*
> *and given the name*
> *Turbot.*

From this day forth she may cross the Equator
in our coral galleon.
Signed: Ship's captain & Neptune.

CHAPTER TWO

Tall tales

I'd sometimes imagined myself with her on the *Europa*, my love-hatred being a powerful stimulus to the imagination. She'd always resented my own independent travels. How tempting to tease her, to tell her tall tales, how in Siberia, where since the collapse of the Soviet Union mosquitoes had grown to the size of crows, I'd traveled in a glass-bottomed boat across Lake Baikal and seen her among the sturgeon gazing up at me. How in Daub where she was born I'd seen Karl, the last emperor of Austro-Hungary, ride past, and seen her, my mother, a ten-year-old, holding her brother's hand as they watched the high-stepping horses. My mother would have listened fascinated, then shaken her head and said: *Bist du aber blöd!* What an idiot you are!

(In fact, I didn't tease her much. Too risky!)

As I looked through the souvenirs of her *Europa* voyage, I could imagine her on board, sour and angry, complaining about the Germans on the ship: *Solche Schweine, die fressen nur Kaviar,* what pigs, all they eat is caviar! The Teutonic revelry around her on the high seas, the lavish consumption, the display of wealth had humiliated her. She'd traveled with her friend, the Baroness, but had felt bitter and missed Otto.

Still, I won't stay overnight in the flat! Where would I sleep? In my mother's bed, God forbid! But I'll take home *Satyr and Nymph.* And I'll take the Meissen bowl. My mother, so adroit at needlework, had glued it clumsily after I had broken it: better to have thrown the pieces away.

I drove home through the park and pulled up by the lake. The leaden expanse of water glimmered in the late afternoon sun. I gazed at the hypnotic play of light and felt full of sudden silent laughter. Suddenly I was alarmed. Had I locked, had I even shut the front door to my mother's flat?

CHAPTER THREE

The Body's Cargo

I'd brought her cornflowers, her favourite, it must be
Mother's Day. Their blue reminds her of her childhood, of
the fields by Daub. I waited, on that day or another, I rang,
I banged on the door. I called: Mother!

What use is the key, if I must stand like this outside her
bolted door! When she does open her frailty makes me
ashamed of the battles I fight with her. She's touching and
comical, what with her wild eyes and wilder hair, and she's
reached a very great age. She stares at me. I suspect that for
a moment she has no idea who I am, even hope it, that I'm
well out of the way in the stockroom of her mind, among
other long forgotten objects. I turn away, otherwise despite
poor eyesight she'll read my face. What does it reveal?
Impatience, exasperation? She'll rage, which makes me
tremble. In the kitchen there are arum lilies in the sink.

Who brought you the lilies?

Mrs McGonagle. She is a dangerous woman.

Why?

She brings me flowers, what does she want?

I put the cornflowers in the sink beside the lilies. I
wonder, has she taken her anti-depressants?

8

Her doctor has recently and cheerfully said to me my mother is the cross I must bear. Have I ever seen her smile? He had asked my permission to prescribe anti-depressants without telling her. I'd agreed. He had flattered her outrageously, telling her that a woman as attractive as she who had had two husbands already should find herself a third. I had stood by, waiting for an outburst at his impertinence. On the contrary, the smile he claimed never to have seen spread over her face. He had then told her to take a rosier view of life, like his own grandmother who had survived Auschwitz.

Now out of the kitchen, you! says my mother. Let me cook!

I do as I'm told. After a while I wonder, has my mother forgotten that I'm here? How long will it take to prepare the meal? I call: Can I help?

I go to the kitchen. She isn't there. If she's gone to the bathroom there's a long wait ahead. The Marks and Spencer's chicken in white wine sauce is on the kitchen counter. Do I dare put it in the oven?

Mother, are you all right?

Ich bin im Klo!

As I'd thought, on the loo! Shall I turn on the oven? Why does she behave as if by turning on a switch in her flat I'm causing the disintegration of the building? Whereas the disintegration here is of the personality, mine!

DON'T touch the oven, I say to myself.

In the living room I wait patiently in the penumbra of familiar objects: the long shadows they cast, these paintings, these antiques, these photographs, are from a forgotten and stormy past.

I hear my mother shuffle back. After a while she calls:

9

Open the wine. I go to her in the kitchen. She is lifting a pot from the hob, her withered arms passing over the jets of flame.

Mother! I cried in horror.

Ach, you make me *nervös!* Stand away!

I stood back, out of her way. She reached, bent like a sickle, into the lower oven. Again, her hands pass over the flames. Would she, like the girl that played with matches in *Struwwelpeter*, become a pillar of fire before my eyes? Those cruel moral tales and illustrations, along with *Max und Moritz*, had been my earliest childhood reading, when German had been my only language. Or would the flames burnish my imperishable mother? She was a phoenix already, I decided, or perhaps, considering her shock of hair, an immortal parakeet.

You need a safer oven, I caution, or you'll die like Resl.

That woman, *such* a greedy snake! May she spin like a windmill in her grave!

My stepfather's sister, who had survived the Holocaust, had died of burns aged 83 after falling in her London flat against an open fire. Despite her tragic life and cruel death mention of her always outraged my mother. I watch anxiously as she backs away from the oven, the dish of steaming chicken in her hands. But she lets me wheel the trolley into the living room and set the table.

What a Gargantuan appetite she has! She has a glass of wine too, so it's surely safe to discuss giving me power of attorney, which she will insist on calling power of eternity. I remind her that *she* has said because her memory is going I will need to run her affairs.

How do I know what you will do with me?

Put you in a bin bag.

Ach, bist du blöd! What an idiot you are!

I'll bring you some forms to sign.

(Pause)

And why should I sign?

The subject of money raises my heartbeat. Her offers are invariably the prelude to a seduction that turns sour.

To make it legal.

And then what I have is yours?

Good God no! All it means is that in an emergency...

What emergency!

You might ... fall ill.

To my relief, instead of scorning the very idea, she sighs and says: Yes, get the solicitor to do it.

And you'll sign it?

Yes.

I'm grateful for the good days, so I give her 'quality time'. I fetch the pigskin briefcase that she keeps in her bedroom and spread out the photographs it contains on the table. I know my mother will tell what I've heard a hundred times and more; the death of my grandfather, of my natural father, also Otto; her marriage to my stepfather Otto, a Jew; the trauma of flight, the refugee years. Are these stories, in their mechanical repetition, memories? After a while, if we're both lucky, something will surface, something new.

Here's a photograph of an empty room! Hazy sunlight falls on rows of school benches. My mother conjures a picture for me, a village school in the hamlet of Daub to which the farmers sent their children, where her father is the teacher.

Her voice trembling, now comes a starburst of memory as she recites:

In Jahren alt und Gütern reich,

teilt einst ein Vater sein Vermögen,
selbst unter die drei Söhnen gleich...

(Old in years and rich in estates/ a father once divided his fortune / equally among his three sons...)

Yes, she sighs, I liked poems. She sighs again: I was a terrible pupil, my father threw my doll's house out of the window because I wouldn't learn.

Look at him!

My grandfather, handsome but inexpressive, even forbidding; none of the several photographs of him reveal anything more than this. Most of them are of the hunt! He stands against a background of forest with his fellow huntsmen, the baron and Franz. There are variations of this theme, different huntsmen, but always at their feet a slain stag.

I find a delightful photograph, the only one that exists of my mother and Franz as children. Look at you, Mother!

Her blonde plaits glisten. She squints into the light. Beside her stands a stick of a boy with close-cropped hair, bony-kneed in baggy short trousers, his arm possessively round his little sister's shoulders.

How old were you?

Ach, I don't know! I had a beautiful childhood! Not many are so lucky.

We are now in the deep well of time, my mother and I. The late afternoon light comes through the window. My legs have grown heavy, my arms hang like broken branches. Have I drunk too much again? Or is the room overheated? What, still only 4:15? Who had given her that clock? Marble, astride it a gilded Cupid about to fly.

My mother gets up, one hand to the small of her back, the other clinging to a chair. Wait, she says, I want to give you something, and leaves the room

I go to the window. The trees are a fiery yellow, the golden shades of whisky. My mother comes back. I've lost it, she wails. It's gone!

Gone?

Is it because she knows I'll soon leave? It's then she tries to delay me by saying she's lost something or other, her glasses, her stick, and now, her money.

Ach Gott, you must find it. And take the lilies when you go! The tears well up, not the wily, hot tears of temper, but a confessional flood. *Ach Gott*, what have I done?

A stooped figure, suddenly she reminds me of my grandmother as without another word she leaves the room. Should I help her to the bedroom? Will she fall? After a while the shuffling stops, I hear a door shut.

She'd hardly have left money in the desk. Too obvious. Still, I looked. Where could it be? Mistrust was my mother's lodestar: *You never know what might happen!* Hadn't the Nazis closed the bank accounts of Jews, and the English were no better with their taxes, or she might never have retired to Switzerland. Better to have your money somewhere safe! I ruled out the kitchen where the long-suffering, but never to be trusted Mrs McGonagle was increasingly in charge.

That left the bedroom.

My mother is asleep and I'm afraid I'll wake her. Her sharp profile, her wild hair over the pillow, the rise and fall of her breath. Would her dying be like this?

A reproduction of Degas's *The Milliner* hangs above the bed. On the chest of drawers are photographs of my children. By her dressing table the photograph of Franz. To the right a small crucifix, beside it in a gilded frame the pressed flowers I had picked for her at Blattendorf.

My mother's face is stern, her snores determined, as if by the sheer force of her personality she intends to elbow out of her way the obstacles confronting her in the sleep into which she's plummeted. I was looking at a frightened old woman. Two images of my mother, the fierce and the frightened, have always been hard to reconcile. I told myself, as if doubting the possibility: *This is my mother.*

The snores become louder. Her deep inhalations and exhalations are like a sea swell crashing on pebbles. She'll not wake now for many hours and any memory of my visit will probably be wiped out.

It rained hard as I drove home. The car's headlights struck a tunnel in the dark and the yellowed leaves swept down to stick briefly to the windscreen. The heady scent of Mrs McGonagle's arum lilies flooded the car.

That night I couldn't get to sleep. Insomnia has plagued me for years. When I was a student I'd take sleeping pills but then I'd go to a jazz club: then how sweetly slow and smooth, how wild the music flowed. Now I always take them after I've visited my mother.

What is the body's cargo, if not memory?
What is desire, if not memory?
Am I still awake?

The dark morning presses against the window, mysterious but not unfriendly. I feel a gentle longing, a confidence in this mothering half-light of the day about to begin. Days began like this once, and they begin again like it now. What I remember feels like love: like those Russian dolls where one contains another, about me are shell upon shell of safety, and what is the universe, what is infinite space to a child, if not the last warm cover?

CHAPTER FOUR

Early Colours

My first memories are surely acts of self-creation. Can I vouch for the accuracy of this first episode where red plays so strong a part, as does sexuality, dubious forger of identity? The little boy, as I see him, is naked. If not, it hardly matters. Unobserved I certainly was, or I wouldn't have been able to take the spool of *red* thread from the workbox and do with it what I then did. However, another colour clamours loudly for attention, or rather delicately, but persistently, show-offishly, as that's the style of the *blue* hydrangea which grows in a tub in my mother's showroom.

Show! What was there to see? Why, modernity! The Cubism of the furniture, the cocktail jazziness of the lacquered screen! Here, before a mirror, the industrialist's wife runs hands over hips to smooth a dress, here a future film star of the Third Reich, the year is circa 1935, dazzles my mother with her youthful Nordic beauty. Yes, I remember the *blue* flower ...

Here the women try on hats.

Here I try my infantile experiment with bondage. How can I forget? I'm enchanted by my reflection in the mirror! I remember *myself.* I had wound the *red, red* thread tightly round my finger, unwound it and seen the marks it left, now I wound the red, red thread round my penis, which became as firm as my finger.

I ran to mother, crying because of the pain. Did she look at the little red twig in amazement and try not to laugh? Then as she performed the delicate operation of cutting me free with her scissors, did she really warn me: I shall cut it off!

There are photographs of me sitting on a pot screaming with rage. *If I don't want to, then I won't!* What is the kingdom I'm defending, if not the integrity of the body? In the harsh climate of the moment, I will not open my hole. *Why should I?* I'm going to hang on a bit to everything that's nicely inside me. Is this revenge for the scissors? Or has some other confrontation sent our wills, like boiling stratocumulus, into the azure sky of the mother-son relationship?

Where is my father? It happens suddenly, it only took a week, says my mother, septicaemia. He asks her not to bring me to the hospital because his face, swollen and monstrous, will frighten me. Death means nothing, only the gradual accumulation of *their* tears and *their* silences carries weight. I absorb these tears, these silences: is it possible that after so many years their grief is still in me? My father's hands touched me, I must have liked that. If I heard a voice in another room, if it was his I must have recognised it. *Did forgetting begin immediately?*

Trees in sunlight, washed by the wind. Giants of stone, one holding a key, another a book, another a cross, look out over the trees, down on a landscape of undulating hills, partly forested, and over fields through which the sleepy Ondra winds its way, sometimes hidden, sometimes silver. Under the trees a rug is spread. Glasses shine on the rug, so does an apple. My mother points: *Schau, Peter!* Look! There, where the pigeons have just flown from the stone heads of the saints to beyond the fields, beyond the dreamy river, to where the forest becomes dense, the tree trunks red among the green-black branches, no further away than the pigeons' flight but already across the border, is *Deutschland.*

Meanwhile in England in 1935: Vernon Bartlett, MP and journalist, after 40 minutes with Hitler in his study, remembers Hitler's 'large brown eyes - so large and so brown one might grow lyrical about them if one were a woman'.

July 1937. Neville Chamberlain tells Ivan Maisky, Soviet Ambassador to Britain: If only we could sit down at a table with the Germans and run through all their complaints and claims with a pencil, this would greatly relieve all tension.

The Viennese waltz is heady and the trout swim, lithe and condemned, in the tank as if in harmony with the music. My mother and my soon-to-be stepfather Otto have each selected one to be served *au bleu.* My mother tells Otto about her father, the village schoolteacher. His love of nature, his strictness, his passion for hunting, his grief at the disintegration of the Empire, his detestation of the Czechs. She had adored him even though he had a temper. In a rage because at fifteen she still played with dolls, he had taken

17

her doll's house and thrown it out of the window. Does Otto wonder as he listens what reception this father would have given him? Does he now talk of his family? They are appalled, most of all Otto's sister Resl, that he plans to marry a gentile, even worse, a widow with a child.

Otto mentions Prague. *Ach Prag!* My mother tries to convey her enthusiasm for cosmopolitan cities. Her small showroom reflects her dreams of a world she calls Monte Carlo or Paris or Biarritz, while in her home town the swastika flies at every window.

The bottle of Moselle is empty; with the dessert, wild strawberries, they each have a coffee and a brandy. Meanwhile Viennese waltzes create their own landscape as surely as a river in flood.

In 1938 Lord Halifax, Secretary of State for Foreign Affairs, looks into Hitler's eyes, 'which I was surprised to see were blue'.

The scene, as my mother tells it, takes place in the village of Bölten, in her mother's kitchen. I can imagine it: the summer heat, the light of storm clouds, on the walls my grandfather's hunting trophies, the antlered skulls and stuffed birds, fierce-eyed emblematic guardians of the purity of the Sudeten German community. A suspicion of her dead father's disapproval makes my mother rebellious. Woven into her sense of oppression are threads of another colour, shame at her brother Franz. He is pleading with his sister not to marry a Jew. *These are dangerous times.*

Otto's family come from the small town of Porlitz in South Moravia where they own a general store. Otto and his younger brother David both studied law in Brno as their father decreed. Otto's sister Resl learned to play the piano a little and married the man chosen for her, a doctor. Otto has received an unsigned letter from Resl who has a son two or three years older than me. She writes: *Will you let the whore lay a cuckoo's egg in our nest?*

Otto's family refuse to meet my mother. Otto's brother is sent to offer my mother money to give up Otto. Otto's father is dying. Otto doesn't want to see him. In the end he goes to his father's deathbed: my mother insists.

1938. I'm in lederhosen, a Tyroler jacket, a shirt and tie, legs braced and hands in pockets, a cocky five- year-old in the mythic Sudetenland. I'm still a German boy. There are other photographs of me with my 'new' father. I look angelic and Otto beams at me warmly. It's a romance.

I want a swastika, the other children have one! My mother gives in, I get my way. A brick has come in through our window. The industrialist's wife will no longer speak to my mother. Other customers stay away.

The frames of my stepfather's glasses are black. His nose is big. Between his eyes and mine, his face and mine, is a newspaper. The newspaper is there like a wall. *There's no point in a father like this!* I throw a shoe at him and it rips the paper. He doesn't say anything. His anger is in his lips which suddenly frighten me. Later he'll say: You were only a child, I decided never again to lose my temper with you. Not long after this he disappears. *Where is he? Is he dead?* I demand to know. He's gone to America, says my mother.

My grandmother keeps bees. The honey is as dark and

sticky as the flypaper she hangs above her kitchen table. I wait for a fly to get stuck in the strange smelling brown glue and buzz angrily as it tries to get free. It's a champion way to catch flies. *Is that all?* A spiral of sticky paper hanging above a table? Why once again am I remembering only things, a place? Is it because everything embodies my grandmother Omi so that while she seems absent her spirit is in fact everywhere, in the room filled with summer heat, the dusty rays of sunlight, the narrow yard, the dusty path outside, heat and dust, and trees and under them on stilts the white beehives? Flypaper, beehives, pots of honey and Omi soon vanish from my life. The word *Bölten* though will remain magical for me for a while yet, an open door until it finally closes to all that *had come before*.

Meanwhile in Britain a British citizen at his own cost publishes and distributes a pamphlet: *The Divine Voice in the Czechoslovakian Crisis of 1938.* (Cost: one penny). Never, the author begins, *in the entire history of the nation has there been an occasion when 'presentiment', 'conviction', 'inner faith' - call it what you will - was so widespread among the peoples as now in connection with the Czechoslovakian Crisis.* In the pages that follow, Czechoslovakia, 'a faraway country of which we know nothing', is not mentioned again. The anonymous author of the pamphlet exhorts the nation, in the face of the deepening crisis, to dedicate itself afresh to the Christian faith and pray.

The Munich Agreement, in which Britain and France allow Hitler's Germany to annex the mainly German populated borderland areas of Czechoslovakia, is signed on September 1938. Czechoslovakia loses one third of its territory. The Sudetenland, as the annexed regions are known, becomes a part of the Third Reich. As a result we find ourselves at shortest notice living in Germany.

My dead father's older brother says he will not allow his nephew to have a Jewish stepfather. Under the Nuremberg Race Laws that now apply I can be taken from my mother. She lets it be known that she plans to divorce her Jewish husband. She takes a train across the new frontier. *The handsome Aryan swine of a frontier guard* asks her where she's going. To visit my mother, she says. But she's not visiting her own, but my stepfather's. She has banknotes of Czech crowns stuffed inside her corset. She's rescuing what she can of Otto's family's fortune. After the sudden death of Otto's father, the family, except for Resl, have accepted Otto's marriage to a Gentile. However my mother drives a hard bargain. She'll emigrate with Otto, it's now only a question of getting visas. She expects Otto's mother to compensate her. A, says my mother, sticking up a thumb: for the loss of her millinery business. B, and up goes her index finger: for what lies ahead. How will they live in England? She intends to set herself up in business, but she needs to arrive with the tools of her trade. And C, and now my mother's hands make fists and drop onto her lap: Otto's inheritance (though Otto had forsworn it when his father refused to allow the marriage) must be put into an account in England in my mother's name as well as Otto's, as for her sake as well as mine she needs to know she's independent. Otto's mother agrees, relieved her son's safety is in capable hands. She herself and Otto's unmarried brother, David, decide to stay in Czechoslovakia. Resl's husband, Dr Borger, considers the possibility of Palestine.

Shortly after this she again leaves Jägerndorf, this time with me. She takes as much, or as little, luggage as seems right for the holiday in Switzerland she tells people she's taking. She can't trust even her oldest friends with the truth, only Omi and Franz know. We're joining Otto in Brünn. (This the German name, the Czech is Brno.)

CHAPTER FIVE

Brünn 1938-1939

Suzie's hair and her large round eyes are dark. Whether I remember this or know it from a photograph, I can't be sure. I draw nearer to memory contemplating the photograph which is now on my desk, so that again feelings of warmth somehow conjure her to life. We're walking down a street holding hands. An elderly woman approaches. I *remember* the pavement, see the two children that stand here, as if circumscribed by a magic circle, *see* a figure that leans into this circle as the woman bends down to us and asks a question: *Are you children Jews?*

I don't know what a Jew is, except I know Suzie is one, and so is my stepfather. I reply as my mother instructed me, should I ever be asked this question: *Ich bin Vollarier aber Sie können mich am Arsch lecken,* I'm totally Aryan but you can lick my arse! My mother, walking a few paces behind with Otto and friends (Suzie's parents?) asks why was the woman upset? I tell her what I said. My mother again gives me a little swastika to wear on the lapel of my jacket. But I still don't know what Jew means, or for that matter Aryan.

March 1939. The German tanks arrive in Brünn early one morning and we've still not got our visas. Now it's not only permission to enter England that we need, but permission to leave the Protectorate, as the occupied country has become under German rule. Too late now to transfer money to accounts abroad! My mother bribes lavishly for the exit permits, there's no hiding now that she plans to leave with a Jewish husband. Meanwhile in England a sponsor has to be found: the Quakers voice deep shame at Britain's betrayal of the Czechs and they come to the rescue. The visas are granted late in July. Otto's family cling to the conviction that it's best to stay where they are.

Good and evil as in a fairy tale. What threatens my stepfather is evil. As a child I understand evil, it is from evil we are fleeing and from evil that my 'new' father needs to be protected. Evil has driven us from our home. All that has come about in our lives is because for Otto's sake we are fleeing from evil.

It would become a part of the myth of that sea journey, our crossing of the North Sea, where unreality made the sky both a serene blue and filled it with clouds in turmoil, where the sea was calm as if in a dream while the ship pitched and all three, the man, the woman and the child vomit; where there are crisp stars in an inky void, but at the same time the sun, or perhaps it was the moon, rolled across the sky, that there was a suicide on this voyage. There will be different versions of this story, all told by my mother later: It happened! It never happened! It was a woman, she threw her own child, then herself, into the sea. And finally: I don't remember! You imagined it! . . . In the

24

radio play I would write decades later for the BBC the boy on this voyage has become a girl: I am Gretl. Free of my boy's body, the future (which for me is already the past) takes a different course: I escape to the female.

A gale is blowing. The creaking ship heaves and rolls, and to these sounds the studio technician adds the lonely cry of a gull. Gretl's question, breathed timidly into the microphone, is barely audible above this medley of sea sounds: When I get to England, will I be English?

CHAPTER SIX

Memory as Landscape

The year: 1989. I'd been corresponding with Josef. He writes to my mother perhaps twice a year. He informs her of family events and sends photographs to which she responds with mixed feelings.

They think in the West we are all millionaires. Why else do they invite you? I try to say something about roots. About family.

What family? The Czechs?

Of course.

You have never met them!

I lay a photograph on the table, a trump card: the chapel in Karlsbruhn, the mountain spa in the Alt-vatergebiet where my mother and father had married.

My mother sighs. When we were marrying you could hear the waterfall. The reception was at a very smart hotel, the Redl.

It won't be called the Redl now.

Ach, if only it still stands!

It may have fallen down.

This makes her angry. I am not an idiot. I know what history is.

What, mother?

A punishment. –*Erst die Nazis. Dann die Kommunisten.* Who knows, perhaps goodbye *die Kommunisten*.

My mother, her eyes wide, gasps: Goodbye *die Kommunisten*!

I'm going, and that's that!

Ach, you get on people's nerves. She jabs the photograph with her finger. Like your father. And you drink. So be careful how you drive!

I had avoided Germany for decades. The signs along the road stirred me, words emblazoned in neon signs, the red loops, the luminous green, the white dots, the blues and harsh yellows of *German words:* they were like flowers remembered from childhood. We had been driving through technicolour German villages, the houses a sparkling white, red geraniums banked at every window. We were now in open countryside, my wife, my son, my daughter and I, on a deserted country road. We came to a simple barrier: this was the Czech-German border.

A young soldier, red-faced on this hot afternoon, waved us on to a low building among the trees. This was 'Kontrol'. As stated in my passport, I had been born in this country. That raised no welcoming smile. I had come in search of a world that had disappeared long before these already middle-aged guards were born. Their dour faces suggested lives set in concrete.

Beyond 'Kontrol' what I could see as we waited in the car was cast in the mould of the ordinary, trees and beyond them water, a river or a lake. I had a moment of misgiving. Was my journey misconceived?

Our passports checked, we are allowed to proceed. Do

I expect something extraordinary to happen as I drive across the border to the magical land of childhood? The sky over this Bohemian landscape is a delicate, smoky blue, fragile as porcelain. On the roadside are young people, dark haired and tawny, Gypsies probably, carrying towels, perhaps they are on their way to bathe. There are glimpses of water beyond the trees. In the fields the hay had been made into stacks as ramshackle as the cottages we pass.

Memory is the landscape I am in. How I wish I could press the blank page of my notebook to the sky to absorb its strange light, to record what beguilingly still seemed the beginning of the day, record images that conveyed the silence and emptiness around me, the patchwork of golden fields and dark forest, and the rowan along the roadside, the branches heavy with clusters of bright red berries.

I sensed a past.

We drove through Cheb. Guidebooks tell of the former glory of this town; for centuries it bore the German name of Eger.

Crumbling buildings: the colours of the forgotten.

An image presents itself: the long narrow form of Czechoslovakia tilted like a games board. The pieces that slide from it and make the game pointless for me are the Sudeten Germans (or rather, their absence), of which the country rid itself in the mass expulsions of 45/46. Under Communism Slovakian Gypsies had been settled in the abandoned farmsteads.

The road descends to the spa of Karlovy Vary. Cement dust blows into the car; perhaps it comes from the decaying grandeur of the nineteenth century hotels. Resl had worked here after the war as a laundress. This was during the two years that she waited for permission to emigrate from Communist Czechoslovakia to Britain.

Soon we are in open country again. The road lies between still sunlit fields set against forests of a green almost black. The land rises, lifting us into the evening sky. Ancient mountain ash line the road, their berries a beacon to an anticipated happiness. I had surely always loved this tree because it belonged to the magical world of my 'Sudeten' childhood. Or are the clusters of bright berries warning me that I'm now travelling in the dangerous and enchanted world of memory?

CHAPTER SEVEN

England 1939

Hedges, trees and fields stand out in vivid shades of green. This is somewhere in England. What my mother and stepfather are discussing a few paces behind me on this country road is intense and private and remains a part of this overcast day, like the thistles by the roadside that I swipe with my stick. A hedgehog crosses the road but I make no attempt to draw my parents' attention to it because they are in a world of their own to which I do not belong. My stepfather had made a suggestion, my mother will one day tell me: *Let's kill ourselves.*

We had been boarded on a farm in Suffolk. My parents were to work here in return for their keep. Due to the lack of a common language, misunderstandings soon arose. The farmer, according to my mother, was *primitiv*. He kept coals in the bath and he wanted to know, why wasn't she wearing a Czech folk costume?

There was a pig on the farm. I'd feed it handfuls of stuff I picked. The farmer slapped me for this, my mother said he had no right, so the farmer slapped her and my stepfather threw up his hands to the sky: or so the story goes. That's the reason we're now walking deeper into the gloom of a rainy English winter afternoon. My parents had walked out in outrage, without taking even an umbrella. My stepfather may have been thinking of suicide but my mother surely was thinking of hats. She has the tools of her trade, a trunk full of crimping irons, felts, veils, feathers, needles and thread, but she needs civilisation, because only there do people wear hats. In fact, only London will do.

A different season: sunshine and clouds. We're on another farm. *Kultivierte Menschen*. Educated people, live here. After this a tunnel lies ahead, or have I already passed through it: separation for weeks or months from my parents. I go to a village school and stay with a Miss Mason in her cottage and remember nothing of any of this. All memories have been erased as a summer storm washes away a hot summer's dust from the trees. When I come out of the tunnel I speak English, my parents definitely don't.

My mother and stepfather rent a room in London, I go to a boarding school on the south coast. On grey afternoons I keep watch at a bay window. I imagine my mother coming down the drive, hear her footsteps on the gravel, know the clothes she'll be wearing, the brown coat in the strange rubbery velvet material, imagine the moment when she comes into sight from behind the shrubs with the waxy yellow-green leaves... I'm alone at the bottom of the garden. Something speckled brownish-yellow stirs at my feet, I almost step on it. Is it *Frosch*, is it *Schlange* that now slide into my thoughts? Are these words I still know? A frog is being swallowed by a snake, it peers from the snake's jaws like a fat man leaning out of a window. The frog's eyes bulge, they're like dark marbles. *Frosch* and *Schlange* belong, immense and magical, to the Sudeten world of *Märchen,* of fairy tale, to Bölten where there are beehives and a room where there are pots of honey. They belong to Omi, perhaps for a moment she stands beside me. *Frosch* and *Schlange* don't stir. Shadows lengthen, the sky darkens to a smudged blue. A bell rings. I run back into the house.

St Leonard's-on-Sea is having its first experience of war, the word 'Krieg' that comes curt and hard from my parents' mouths; in English 'war' sounds almost like a yawn.

If we weren't in the middle of an air raid, says Mr Roberts, I'd tell you to go back and put slippers on your feet. The Anderson shelter in the garden is under a mound of earth and inside there's a smell of mouldering leaves. Mrs Roberts brings in a tray with cups of cocoa.

The trees are lit as if by a giant hand holding a flaming torch. This is a burning Messerschmitt that narrowly misses the school before it crashes further down the road. The blast makes the trees heave and toss. *I saw this with my own eyes, no really, I did!*

Back to your beds, says Mr Roberts. We run barefoot through the wet grass to the house and leap into our beds but it's already getting light.

Why is Mrs Roberts so fat, I'd asked my mother on her visit. She and Otto had smiled teasing smiles, but as I got no answer I remained disastrously ignorant of the 'facts of life'. Not long after the air raid Mrs Roberts got puzzlingly thinner.

Come and see the baby, says Mr Roberts. Mrs Roberts shows us the baby. Its fists are clenched, its fingers like the new-born mice in the cage in the playroom.

I'm one of only two Catholics at Mr Robert's School, the other is Oh Yea Alakijah. Where Oh Yea is from I don't know, he's black. I'm short for my age and he's immensely tall. Walking to church with Oh Yea along the water front we saw a German submarine collide with a mine and explode ... *We saw it with our own eyes, no really, we did!*

Confirmation or excommunication, Oh Yea and I are being prepared for one or the other. I have a memory of white lacy gowns, silver dishes, smoking incense. A priest lays his hand on my head.

There's also confession. Now, I'd stolen a bar of chocolate from an unlocked tuck box. I expected my confession to bear fruit, even make it eagerly. The father confessor asks me if I know my Hail Marys. Yes, I lie. Say a dozen, says he. I left the confessional and knelt in front of an altar. I simulate prayer, but I'm puzzled: Why wasn't I told to return the chocolate? Or if I'd eaten it, buy another bar?

I don't remember ever replacing the chocolate. Whatever the case, after this I no longer feel a need to take seriously a Father, Son and Holy Ghost. Scepticism or cynicism, depth or shallowness?

What do you think, Oh Yea?

Didn't you see the hand of God, Peter, reach out of the sky? Oh Yea! Oh Yea!

Peter! Peter!

(Exeunt)

CHAPTER EIGHT

Photographs

Our new flat in Abbey Road has two rooms. My parents' bedroom, where I am, is where my mother's customers try on hats. The other small room is where my mother and Mary make the hats. Mary is English and my mother employs her.

My parents have gone to the building opposite where Oskar Busch *hat sich umgebracht.* I more or less know what that means. Oskar Busch has killed himself. My parents' shocked faces, their whispered German had told me.

Before going out my mother gives me a small suitcase full of photographs for me to look at of our life back in the *Sudetenland.*

Keep away from the window! Don't touch the curtains. If any light shows the police will think we're spies and we'll all go to prison.

The photographs are spread out on my bed. Of my mother there are many; in a white beret, white blouse, white silk stockings and white pleated skirt, leaning against the bonnet of a white Mercedes. In white silk pyjamas under palms in a conservatory. With her terrier Struppi that had snapped at me in my cot. Of Omi there is one of her scowling in her kitchen; behind her on the wall, a clock and the bleached skulls, my grandfather's trophies from the hunt. There are three photographs of my *real* father. One my mother had cut from his passport after his death. His face is almost blotted out by the official stamp. Another is of him in a wide-brimmed hat in the cemetery in Jägerndorf by his parents' grave. The one I like best is of him at seventeen, handsome in a white uniform. He'd lied about his age to enlist in the Austro-Hungarian army. Not long after this photograph was taken he was blinded in his right eye by a fragment of shrapnel. That was on the Italian front at Garda. There's a photograph of my stepfather's sister Resl with her son, a boy my age with a large head, cropped hair and ears that stick out.

Outside the cone of light from the bedside lamp loomed the cabin trunks, the boxes of felts, ribbons, artificial flowers and veils my mother had brought with her to make hats.

When are my parents coming back?

Just then the doorbell rings. I'm frightened ... The bell rings again. After a while I hear footsteps recede in the corridor, not the tap tap of my mother's high heels, but shoes that squeak. The lift door opens and shuts and the lift rattles down.

Who was it?

I run to the window, push my head between the curtains and peer out. The street is deserted, the moon shining. I wait: directly below the window is the entrance to our building, Langford Court. A boy comes out of the building. He stands a while between the potted shrubs at the entrance, then crosses the street and goes into the building where the unhappy Mr Busch, because he'd had to say goodbye to his wife at the *Grenze* and come to England on his own, *hat sich umgebracht.*

CHAPTER NINE

Wales

At the new school whatever intelligence I possess evidently drains from me. My hands under the desk take on a life of their own. I flip them at the wrist as if I had a nervous disease. They carry things to my mouth, pencils, erasers, which I chew. I bite into a glass retort. Pleeth thir, I try to explain, through a mouth thick with blood and broken glass, I'm hurt!

I'm a different child outdoors. . . I become observant of plants, of birds, of rocks; with time, after more tearful separations from my mother, I've learned that what remains, what can be depended on, is nature. Memories come to me of that childhood world, sensations of touch and smell; the pine needle floor of the woods, flowers and fungi; crumbling wood swarming with lice; the light on water.

I'm fishing. The eel glides from its hiding place in the underwater roots of a tree and swallows the baited hook. There's an explosion of bubbles as the eel struggles fiercely. I've got it. I take out my pocket knife to slice off its head. The headless eel oozes a frothy slime and twists itself into knots.

Mount Tryfan looms, majestic in fiery storm cloud. I've wrapped the eel in a dock leaf. I'm going to give it to Mabel, the cook, who's told me she'll eat it. I run with it through fields where sheep are grazing. They stare at me with melancholy eyes. The sun is sliding down the grey back of Mount Tryfan. It's getting late, I'll be in trouble.

Go on, says Mabel. Tell us another!

It's true, Mabel! The woman threw her baby overboard.

Why would she do that, Peter?

Because they didn't have a visa.

A VISA! Honestly, Peter, you do tell fibs!

It happened on the ship when we came to England, Mabel. It really did! The woman was going to jump into the sea, but people stopped her. The baby drowned.

Well, I must say! Now help me peel the spuds, Peter!

Mr Murray gives beatings with his belt and uses the buckle end. Mr Goodwin's beatings are more like being tickled. He puts one hand between your legs and feels you, while he slaps your bare bottom gently with the other. I've had beatings from Mr Goodwin and Mr Murray.

What have you been up to today, Peter?

Nothing, sir.

Nothing! That's not very much.

I caught an eel, sir.

Did you now! I hope you signed in?

Oh... I forgot, sir!

We can't send search parties combing the mountains for children who are just plain forgetful, Peter! What's the book for? Be in my room at eight!

Yes, sir.

At least Mr Goodwin's beating won't hurt.

The signing-in book is kept in the hall. How else can the understaffed school keep track of so many children? Once lessons are over we're free to roam. (That no boy drowned or vanished for ever in the dripping and deep tunnels of the disused and out-of-bounds quarries is little short of a miracle.) The village rarely saw a car, and not many walkers apart from us boys, lined up in a crocodile to be marched to church on Sundays and twice a week to the village hall to see films with Will Hay and George Formby, and once a wonderful and spooky film in a haunted house with Bob Hope, *The Cat and the Canary.*

One memory comes with tantalising clarity: the Conway river formed a pool in which we children bathed. We'd dash naked across the road, waving our towels, and scamper down the riverbank. The pool was wide and mostly shallow, with a rock that stuck out of the water like the back of a porpoise. I'd stand on the rock and watch the slow, darkly shining water divide as it flowed past. I can still see the dark pebbles, the darting stickleback, sometimes a trout, in that magic world under the pane of water through which the sun shone brightly onto the river bed. On that rock I'd sailed naked through the world. Wholeness belongs to that time when as a boy I had stood on the rock as if on the prow of a ship and in my imagination had gone on fantastical journeys. The river grew wider, the shore disappeared from sight, vast was the ocean. On Sundays in the chapel a bright light shone on the stained glass of St George, whose lance I plunge into the neck of the Dragon.

There was a bookcase full of books from the school's hotel days. I found a book here that I would read with guilty fascination and many years later found it again in the Reading Room of the British Museum:

The time being come when the innocent mother with her two daughters should suffer, in the place where they should consummate their martyrdom were three stakes set up. At the middle post was the mother, the eldest daughter on the right hand, the youngest on the other. They were first strangled, but the rope broke before they were dead, and the poor woman fell in the fire. Perrotine, who was great with child, did fall on her side, where happened a rueful sight not only to the eyes of all that there stood, but also to the ears of all true-hearted Christians that shall read this history. For as the belly of the woman brast asunder by the vehemency of the flame, the infant, a fair man child, fell into the fire, and being taken out of the fire by one W. He was laid upon the grass. Then was the child had to the provost, and from him to the bailiff, who gave censure that it should be carried back again and cast into the fire. And so the infant baptised in his own blood, to fill up the number of God's innocent saints was both born and died a martyr, leaving behind to the world, which it never saw, a spectacle wherein the whole world may see the Herodian cruelty of this generation of Catholic tormentors, ad perpetuam rei infamiam.

I didn't want to be caught reading this book. I kept it hidden in the room that was usually the emptiest, the 'quiet room', where I'd push it inside an old torn sofa. One evening Mr Murray leaned over my shoulder and took the book out of my hands and looked at the title: *Foxe's Book of Martyrs.*

MUST I REPEAT! INTO YOUR BEDS AND SILENCE! And silence there is when Mr Murray is on patrol, except for 'Peter and the Wolf' or 'The Teddy Bears Picnic' or best of all, ITMA.

It's that man again! It's Tommy Handley!

Here they come, Mrs Mop, *Can I do you now, sir?* Ali Oop, Vodkin, Prattle, Sam Scram, the Mer, *I decler,* Funf the Spy and Farmer Jollop ... The weekly radio programme, England's laughing answer to the Führer, is relayed over speakers in the corridors to us in our beds. Even the moon at the window grins.

Please please please please ... every night, not only because it is *almost* the only prayer I know, but because it's the strongest, better than 'Our father which art in Heaven', depending though how often I say *please,* a hundred times probably won't grant a wish. I've so many wishes, but really they're all the same: to go home... this wish, made of so many others, allows me for a while to see my mother's face very clearly. All that I'm wishing for is concentrated in these moments before finally I grow sleepy from praying *please* a hundred times, five hundred times, I keep count of the hundreds on my fingers and have set myself a target of a thousand ...

Then blue... so blue... softly through the speakers sweeps the Danube... The homesickness waltz... blue... so blue. It comes from far away, from somewhere outside, from the dark branches tossing in the wind, the moon riding the clouds. Mr Murray stands in the doorway and holds up his belt. The clouds drift past, blown by the music. The moon in the window lifts me in its white arms and begins to dance with me, over the forest, over the dark water

41

of the lake, above Tryfan. The rat under the floorboards bites the cheese. The spring comes down on its slinky back and snaps its spine. The waltz is over. The window-panes are milky black. Outside the curling fog is thick. Only the snuffle of blocked noses greets the creaking footsteps in the corridor, not a sign of anyone awake in any bed. The boys that so delight Mr Goodwin are all asleep.

CHAPTER TEN

Millions like us

The red welts on my buttocks had still not healed when I came home at the end of term. My mother is amazed the English can do such things to children, but after discussing the matter with my stepfather, they decide not to complain. Were they so conscious of being foreigners, of the risk of speaking out of turn? My mother was anything but timid. If I now compare her to myself, I can see that there was a hard crust of aggression and beneath it a chronic insecurity.

My stepfather, unfit for military service, had been a lawyer. In London he tried to sell 'fancy goods'.

My mother had set herself up as a milliner. If anyone doubts that hats could be a lucrative business in wartime, he need only look at films of the period. Not of course films about factory girls, such as *Millions Like Us* (1943), but *Mrs Miniver* (1942) in which hats frame Greer Garson's regal features, or the hat like a military cap perkily awry, as worn by Celia Johnson in *Brief Encounter* (1945). Cheeky hats, militaristic but feminine, that made a statement: *I'm in charge and don't you forget it!* And straw cartwheels, as worn in countless musicals. And hats worn by the Queen, whether in the East End 'able to look in the face' the East

Enders now that Buckingham Palace too had been bombed, or at some other royal event.

My mother soon established herself as a modish milliner. The wife of an officer in the Free Czech Army recommended her to friends: before long she had enough customers to keep her sewing late into the night. My stepfather meanwhile accumulated 'fancy goods'. By the end of the war we had several boxes of unsold powder compacts, cigarette lighters and lipstick holders.

My mother's employees in our small flat came and went. I was dazzled by Ann with her white skin and flaming red hair, combining the allure of Maureen O'Hara, Maria Montez and Dorothy Lamour. The chronological evidence however suggests I'm overlaying these earlier memories with the glamour of movies I had yet to see: their technicolour excitement floods back over those innocent times.

CHAPTER ELEVEN

Shamed

I was always pestering my stepfather to share a bath with me. The more he looked uncomfortable, the more it became my obsession. *Come in the bath and play.* How old was I? Finally, at last, embarrassed, he said: Get in the bath and wait for me. What can my parents be whispering about outside the bathroom door? When my stepfather comes in, what a shock! He's wearing trunks. Whatever I'd wanted from him, whatever it was, now my attention is drawn to his bathing trunks and their purpose, and without my understanding why, I feel shame. My stepfather's prudery is my humiliation. So I'm granted another year or two of *deadly ignorance.*

CHAPTER TWELVE

A deadly species

In the small flat which during the day is the workroom and showroom I'm in the way. I don't know who first thought to send me on those long bus rides, those time-killing and aimless journeys into the unknown that then, and still now, fill me with fantasy. With a shilling in my pocket, I'm off for the day! I bus-ride to Notting Hill, from Notting Hill to Richmond, to the river bank, the Thames. To Regent's Park, to Kilburn, to playgrounds, to cinemas; alone and back home again at dusk. *Where have I been?* To Australia, where else, on the top deck of the number 13; to Fiji and Tonga and all the pink corners of the British Empire depicted in my stamp album, that still has to be filled with stamps. *And what have I seen?* Icebergs and penguins. Leopards and wolves.

Go to the zoo, says my mother. I identified with the animals in their captivity, I had a physical sensation of their confinement, but it didn't upset me. Did that reflect my own life? Was I prowling in my own cage? I'm mesmerised by the powerful animals, the dangerous, sleek big cats. All comfort is here, and in the apes there's shuddering comedy as well. In their lit glass tanks in the dark Reptile House the creatures fascinate me. I wait patiently for a sign of life, an eyelid to open, a crocodile's nostrils to rise out of the murky water, a snake to unwind its coils and move. Yes definitely, I have an affinity with animals in cages. In fact, there's solace on the days I spend alone at the zoo. Eventually, but not just yet, here I'll encounter the deadly species of paedophile. *Where have you been today?* Then my lies will cease to be the free play of a child's imagination and instead become urgent.

CHAPTER THIRTEEN

Sinking the Bismarck

My mother business was soon a success. She and my stepfather now spent the day in premises they had rented in the West End. During school holidays I was alone in the flat. I love to play with fire. The paper boat I've made floats in the kitchen sink, the *Bismarck*. My hands move quickly as I strike match after match, flames shot from my fingertips. Some bombs fall in the water and go out with a sizzle. Others fall on deck: under the deadly assault the paper blackens, the flames run like spiders, soon all who sail on the *Bismarck* are helpless in a web of fire, revenge for the sinking of the British dreadnought *Hood*. Just as I've seen it happen in newsreels, human lives slip with the uptilted destroyer down into the depths of the Atlantic. Invisible at first, the flames climb the net curtain by the sink, to my horror I see a rope of fire from the ship to the ceiling. I pull the curtain down and douse the flames in the sink. My mother, when she saw the scorched curtain that evening, pressed my finger on the electric hotplate to make sure I understood that fire burns.

CHAPTER FOURTEEN

The war in Europe is over

That scorching summer, the last of the war, I was one of a dozen boys who stayed at the school when the others went home for the summer holiday. I'd gone alone into the forest and flung a match into the bracken, dry as tinder, where gossamer webs trapped the sunlight. Flames shot into the air. Then disappeared in sunlight as the bracken curled into ash. The magic I'd begun leaped up around me, danced behind me, was already in the tree. A wood pigeon calls, ruu ruu ruu. Around me a ring of trees and craggy rocks reach into the sky. The trees divide the sunlight into dazzling rays. Ruu ruu ruu. The pigeon's call echoes from the valley.

That night, or some other, there was a forest fire. The flames snaked down the mountain towards the village. The combustible trees exploded like fireworks. By the time the moon had risen through the drifting smoke, though flames still flared here and there, the danger had passed. The wind had changed direction.

Some nights later those few of us who hadn't gone home for the holidays were woken by the sound of shattering glass. Light danced across the ceiling from a fire outside. We ran to the dormitory windows. Opposite, where the river widens, a bonfire blazes on the rock on which I had not so very long ago voyaged naked round the world. Now men are naked on it singing, or rather yelling 'Roll out the barrel'. Bottles fly through the air and shatter. The men leap from light into darkness, into the river, and clamber out again onto the rock. I watch spellbound by their nakedness. There were bonfires everywhere in Britain that night. The war in Europe is over.

CHAPTER FIFTEEN

1947: An Aryan pedigree and compensation

The problem is the bottle marked: HERZ. He's the 'boy' he likes to remind me, whom I saw leave the building that night when my parents had gone to the building opposite where Oskar Busch had killed himself.

He's allowed his own bottle, my mother accepts his need to drink. First she'll announce to the card players that soon the bell will ring, it will be Herz. I know the shape of her story, her turns of phrases, the inflection of compassion, the moments where she pauses for effect. He's bitter, she'll say, he's lonely, and then there's that other problem, that's why he needs us. Of one thing unfortunately she's certain, it was a mistake to have let him put aside a bottle of whisky for his own use on Friday nights.

Stand behind me and watch, says my stepfather at the card table, trying to encourage an interest in bridge. But I already know that the cards in his hand are depression and silence, trumps against which there's no appeal. Like the bridge players, my stepfather and Herz have lost loved ones in the Holocaust. What grief he felt, how he reacted, will forever remain a mystery. I ask him no questions about the cards in his hand and he offers no explanations. Nor do I volunteer the doubts about my sexuality. We've come to an agreement in the last year or so to leave each other alone. I move away from the card table.

The doorbell rings. Ah ha, says my mother, with an air of I-told-you-so: Herz!

I go to the hall to open the door, but as I leave the room I hear one of the players say: Does Herz shave? Is he a man or a woman, when I see him he always gives me a shock.

How well I remember you, Herz! The way you'd stand there at the door in your shabby raincoat, your whispered question: Who's here tonight?

The usual bunch, I whisper in reply.

Your hand darts to your trilby. You push it back and scratch your head. I'll come another evening.

These bridge evenings in fact are my mother's concession, to bring a little life back into Otto. Until recently, Friday evenings had been reserved for Herz alone, who hates bridge.

My mother, who suspects that Herz is about to leave, shouts from the living room, Herz, be sensible! Come in!

Come to join the men, eh Herz! (Or am I, like Alice falling down the rabbit hole, selecting from the shelves of memory, taking from one bottle of particular interest, labelled: MASCULINITY? Were any of the card players, all male, so insensitive as to greet Herz in this way? Or ask him about his women?

Herz takes out the whisky. He's marked the label to show how much was left after his last Friday visit, or as my mother says, how much he drank. He pours two large glasses.

I shan't keep a bottle for you, Herz, says my mother, if

you teach Peter to drink.

Herz's lips part, a razor smile that reveals small teeth, pearls if they hadn't been so nicotine-stained. My bottle, my prerogative! .

My parents know it's really me Herz comes to see. When all's said and done, he's a *good* influence. So after Herz has had his first whisky, and his coffee's been poured, black please, and the whipped cream heaped onto his *Torte* despite his protest, we leave the living room. Before we go to your room, says Herz, I'd like to pay my respects to your grandmother.

My stepfather had gone to find her in the post-war chaos of displaced people. In the small suitcase which was all she had brought with her she had packed Franz's 'Aryan pedigree', the notorious *Ahnenpass,* a document most Germans had surely thought it wiser to destroy at the war's end.

This document to establish 'racial purity' fascinated me. The pages were bordered in black as if for a bereavement. This seemed appropriate: the *Ahnenpass* was a cemetery of sorts. One might say the future had been buried here. On the grey cover was an embossed eagle bearing a swastika. The blank pages were to be filled with the required genealogical information. For this, there were precise instructions:

Older members of the family will be able to give the places and times of birth, and many other dates of our ancestors, of value to our search. As this information could contain mistakes, as there is not always evidence, it may not be written in ink into the Ancestral Passport. A soft pencil is recommended for temporarily entering these dates.

Had Franz carefully read these instructions? There were no signs of any pencil entries, later erased. Again: *An important aid in setting up the genealogical table is the information obtained from aunts.*

Aunts, according to this text, which Herz helped me translate, being frequently maiden, would have taken a keener interest in family life and better remember life's timetables: whose birth, whose marriage, whose death, when and where? They very likely already had the information one would otherwise need to look for in registry offices, in birth and death certificates, in wills and military passes, even in school reports. Importantly, an aunt might know what one might hesitate to enter even in pencil, let alone ink, regarding those illegitimacies if not forgotten, long concealed, of which it says in the *Ahnenpass*: *If there is absolutely no document to establish paternity, then the matter will have to rest with establishing the Aryan descent of the mother, and the father will be presumed Aryan, if there is no definite indication in the mother's way of life to indicate a non-Aryan father.*

Ideally, ancestry was to be traced back prior to the French Revolution which, according to the *Ahnenpass,* had led to the neglect of the concept of family, clan and *Volk*, by placing the individual above the whole and lifting the restrictions until then imposed upon Jews.

Had Franz thought it unnecessary to fill in more than spaces 4 and 9 *(parents and grandparents),* and left spaces 10 to 63 blank as there was sufficient evidence of his 'Aryan' descent on the tombstones and in the registries of the Moravian village cemeteries where his ancestors of generations lay?

Omi never joins the others on these evenings. My

mother's guests forget she doesn't speak English, or perhaps they speak it instead of German so she shan't understand when they talk about *those things*. Besides, they all smoke like chimneys and as for Mrs Steiner, she kicks off her shoes as if she were in her own flat, and her breasts are always half out of her blouse.

I knock on my grandmother's door. She's not in bed yet, so we go in. She's by the window, reading one of the German novels I find for her, about the old home country, about foresters and forests. Or it could be her prayer book.

Herz asks Omi how she is and she asks him, *how is he?* How should I be, says Herz, and laughs wryly. He understands my grandmother's anger that forbids discussion of the war and *German war crimes.*

I had seen the newsreel of the liberation of Belsen concentration camp shown in cinemas throughout Britain at the war's end. I had asked my grandmother if she had suspected such things. She had been angry. *The Germans did not do such things!* Yet she surely knew enough about Otto's family and their fate. What she thought as the years went by I never discovered. She kept Franz's *Ahnenpass* in a bedside drawer beside her rosary and prayer book..

My grandmother promises Herz that she'll bake him *Streuselkuchen,* the cake he so likes when he comes next Friday. We say goodnight and go to ...

My room!

A unit of dark wood makes up a wardrobe, cupboards, a glassed bookcase and my sofa-bed. This furniture has its history. It had been made to order in Jägerndorf when my parents married. After my mother's marriage to my stepfather and our subsequent flight to England Franz had put it in storage, where miraculously it had survived not only the war but the Czech looting and destruction of German property in the first days of the Liberation. It had been shipped to England and only recently arrived. Though I'd spent the first six years of my life surrounded by this furniture, which had not even needed to be repainted, re-glazed or re-upholstered, it triggered no memories. I'd hidden in the wardrobe, my mother had told me, didn't I remember how I'd annoyed her that day? How I'd had tantrums, stamped my feet? How I'd spilled milk over her and the sofa-bed? How I'd cried in that chair when my father had died? Didn't I remember *anything?* I liked the bed, the desk and the bookcase, but they failed to confirm with a single memory these stories told to me about myself in that *other life*.

I tell Herz about Colin, my school friend, with whom I have a romantic and fiercely antagonistic friendship. My heart begins to pound because I'm suddenly about to confess, but what? Instead I say: I really don't want to learn bridge!

Herz says matter-of-factly: You despise your stepfather.

DO NOT!

Herz's eyes are dark as black coffee. He looks hard at me. Your mother will cut my whisky allowance, he says, if I spend all my time with you. Come instead and visit me one evening!

A silence greets our return to the living room. Then the conversation continues despite the alarmed look on my mother's face. The card players are discussing a dangerous topic, compensation: how much for the loss of a parent, a spouse, a sibling, perhaps even a child; how much for the loss of property; for ruined health; for lifelong despair.

PLEASE, my mother pleads. But it's too late. In the

drama about to unfold, only Herz and I are standing, the others are seated. I'm at the circumference, or more exactly, by the antique desk, by the door that leads to the interior of the flat, and Herz is at the centre of the room, on the Persian carpet, under the sparkling chandelier with its pretty amethyst drops, in his hand a cup of black coffee in which the lights of the chandelier are reflected. With sudden bitterness it bursts out of him: You call yourself Jews!

Not tonight, Herz! My stepfather pleads. PLEASE!

Herz is, in my memory, eternally at the centre of this room, this moment, where all around him now fall silent. He castigates them: You people have no memory. You let yourselves be compensated for everything from the loss of a button to murder! You know the price, that's what's disgusting about you! You're willing to take it from the people who murdered you! You even go back for a holiday!

Every Friday you come here, Herz, every Friday you get drunk and insult us! If we want to go to Austria, that is our right! says my mother. Herz recovers his composure, more or less. His eyes are still wild and fierce. He makes an ironic bow and stumbles from the room to let himself out of the flat.

My mother says to me: Go after him, see he gets home safely! This will be his last bottle, I promise you. Not only has Herz stuck a label on it with his name, but he's written underneath: ONLY PETER MAY DRINK FROM THIS BOTTLE.

CHAPTER SIXTEEN

Troy is taken

I drive on the *new* motorway that cuts through the landscape of my adolescence whenever I visit my mother, perhaps once a week. As I take the flyover by Paddington Station I pass above a tract of wasteland, at the edge of which a building stands, one might think derelict though in fact these flats are still inhabited, and look up at a window. I rarely drive past without some memory of Herz (July 1st, 1909 - April 8th, 1965).

When did I first go to that room? The room of memory, a composite of many visits, is lit by light reflected from glassed bookcases, from leather bindings, from Herz's spectacles, by the light in the glass in his hand in which, as he sways to music on the gramophone, whisky swirls like the fiery liquor of life.

He's listening to *Don Giovanni* on the gramophone. I'm to sit down. He points to the sofa, leaves the room to get a glass, fills it with whisky and puts it in my hand. I'm about to get up. Sit! he says. Sit!

Leporello is singing, counting the women Don Giovanni has had. Six hundred in Italy, two hundred in Germany, and in Spain, oh in Spain, one thousand and three!

On a shelf stands a white crackle-glaze porcelain figure, the Chinese deity of Compassion, one of Herz's favourite pieces. His resemblance to her is striking, not that he has the figurine's elegance, his trousers and his sweater are none too clean. But he has the porcelain goddess's seraphic smile as he listens to the music.

Another whisky?

Soon the floor becomes the sloping deck of a storm-tossed ship. Light from a lamp shines on Herz's latest acquisition, a baroque lime-wood carving of the Creation. God's right hand rests on a globe riddled with woodworm.

British soldiers must have looted it from a German church, says Herz, and somehow managed to get it to England and sold it to a dealer. It cost me twenty pounds, what do you think of that?

How did *you* come to England, Herz?

Herz raises a finger, Ssssh, later! His eyes are shut, the whisky glows. We listen as the drama of seduction and murder, where love and justice triumph. Don Giovanni is dragged into hell. The opera is over.

I'm drunk.

Herz opens his eyes, he's been thinking about my question. Via Poland, he says, thanks to no less a personage than Neville Chamberlain. One of the side effects of the Munich *Diktat,* when, as you no doubt already know the British prime minister secured peace in our time and delivered you and me into the safekeeping of the Führer, one of the side effects of that ignominious treaty was that it ended the treatment I was receiving.

I decide not to reveal my ignorance about the Munich *Diktat.* Nor do I ask about the treatment, but he volunteers:

A few more injections and I might have been a giant. The still experimental treatment had not added a centimetre to Herz's height. Nor, I imagined, any pubic hair to his child's body. The unperceptive take him for a boy of ten, and the malicious for a freak.

Yes, a few more injections!

(*Pause*)

You know, he says, the Germans would have had to gas me twice, once for my size, and then for being a Jew.

(*Pause*)

My mother and I left Jägerndorf and went to Brünn, if you know where that is! You don't! Here's an atlas! Herz takes an atlas from a shelf and drops it in my lap.

In Brünn one misty morning in March 1939 Herz looked out of the window. The country had been invaded overnight. There were German tanks in the street. We had no magic carpet, says Herz, and we still had no visas to allow us into England. My mother said we should put our heads in the gas oven, but I said I'm young! Yes, said my mother, you're young. Go! So I left her and went.

Herz pours two more whiskies. I bounced a ball, my young friend, says he, right to the frontier, and there I gave it a hefty kick. It soared like a Zeppelin, the frontier guard was amazed. I ran to the ball, picked it up, smiled at the guard and said, which way is Poland? - Over there, little boy! - Thank you, I said, gave the ball another kick, ran after it, and that was how I left Czechoslovakia.

And ended up in Albion, Herz?

Where I juggled fifteen oranges, my boy! It was the only way to mesmerise the English into allowing me to enter their country, as I had no visa. (I have a vision of Herz, the juggled oranges like a halo round his head, a magical and luminous figure gliding over the waves to the white cliffs of Dover, where resistance to this foreigner melts like butter on hot toast.)

Herz, I suddenly realise, is quietly crying.

War is declared on 3 September. Herz tries to enlist in whatever army will have him, British or Free Czech. He dreads the medical because he'll have to show himself naked, but it never comes to that. The British recruiting officer takes one look and says, too short, sir! The Czech says, serve us in some other way!

In Jägerndorf Herz had been notorious for his brilliant cartoons. He sketched them on the paper tablecloths of cafés. He lampooned old friends, his pen initially kinder than his tongue, until the day these same childhood friends appeared with a swastika in the lapel of their jackets. These friends kept the coffee- stained caricatures of themselves, which they tore from the paper tablecloth, framed on their walls, until other cartoons began to appear on the tablecloths of the town's restaurants, to the outrage of the town's Nazis. Just days before the Munich *Diktat* he drew a cartoon that provoked the town's citizens to demand he be thrown headlong into the town's synagogue and both set on fire. On 'Kristallnacht' some weeks later the synagogue did indeed burn, but by then Herz and his mother were in Brünn. This cartoon was Herz's parting gift to his birthplace: nannies Chamberlain and Daladier proudly watch the infant Hitler make a bowel movement, his baby feet are in Germany, his buttocks hang over the Sudeten territory of Czechoslovakia, from his anus a lava emission labelled *ein Volk, ein Reich, ein Führer* descends on the town, identified by the twin towers of its baroque church and the faces of its mayor and certain of the town's dignitaries who gaze up in ecstasy at Hitler's arsehole.

Herz now took up his pen again. A weekly cartoon for a Zionist paper helps pay the rent for the one-room flat in which he still lives. A lawyer in Jägerndorf, he sets himself up as a graphic designer. Through chance meetings he learns of the fate of friends.You were two streets away, he tells me. Once I knew where you lived I went round to see you. No one was in, or rather, your front door was open. You were alone in the flat, fast asleep.

At about this time, that's to say in the first months of the war, Herz saw the crackle-glaze porcelain figurine in a junk shop. He bought it with the money he'd intended for a rye loaf and some German-style pickled gherkins. Remember, in those days, refugees travelled across London for rye bread! But when for the same money you could buy a Hokusai print, an ancient Greek vase, a rare old book!

I must have been sixteen when I came to know Herz's room. By then, the walls were crowded with framed maps, engravings, prints and pottery. Between rows of books there are neolithic axe heads, a human skull, Japanese sword handles, a canopic jar from Egypt. Dürer's *Melancholia,* taken from the original block, gazes down. (Her expression suggests piercing thought, like the play of light on ice, everything else about the seated, pondering figure is granite. I was surprised to discover, years later, that *Melancholia* had wings.) In a glass-fronted case are the lekythos, and other vases that he names and explains to me: an oinochoe, a kantharos, an alabastron, and I forget what else. There is pottery from the East. Bowls with glazes of cobalt blue, plum purple and the lovely green of celadon ware.

By his bed are photographs of Herz's mother, his brother, his brother's wife and their children. He plans to bring them to England when the war is over. With this in mind he restrains his passion for collecting and saves. His brother could work with him in his graphics business: Prometheus Limited. He rents a basement office near the British Museum. My first commission, says Herz, was from your mother. A hatbox. She stayed upstairs and sat sewing throughout the Blitz. Your stepfather carried you down to the shelter.

When the sirens wailed Herz would jump out of bed, pull on trousers and sweater over his pyjamas and climb the fire escape to the roof, metal helmet on his head, the strap tight under his chin, to fire-watch. On the roof he feels he's on a ship. Buildings are like rocks he sails past in the fire storm. One night, as London burns, he finds himself thinking of the opening lines of *Agamemnon*. The watchman on the roof of Atreus' palace waits night after night for the beacon flare that will announce the fall of Troy. The city is taken.

The room slopes alarmingly. Herz is the fierce-eyed captain on this ship. The Goddess of Compassion is riding the waves, her moon-face smiling sweetly. The worm-eaten, driftwood God clings to his globe. Herz's own paintings of swirling fiery leaves lean down from the wall. I'm drunk, I need air. I go to the window. A train rattles into Paddington Station. Sparks shoot from its funnel. The sky is clear and the stars are out.

Peter, for God's sake stay sober!

Pass the bottle, Herz!

CHAPTER SEVENTEEN

The price of a life

Herz!... Here he is again! A midget on a lotus, one delicate long-fingered hand raised in a gesture that signifies teaching while the fingers of the other are entwined in a garland of white flowers and delicately hold up a fold of his white robe. Herz's moon-face smiles, but the eyes are dark and hard. He insists that my friendship with Colin is *unnatural*.

Nature didn't treat you so kindly either, I say. Midget! But does that make *you* unnatural?

I've drunk too much again, but that isn't the reason I suddenly feel sick. My heart pounds. I apologise to Herz.

For what, he asks.

For saying what I just did.

We can't defend ourselves, says Herz, by being nice. You want to know who you are. What do I do? I fill you up with drink and preach. You, and you alone may allude to the visible fact of my diminutive stature. But in future do so politely.

Herz and I have spent the evening together, as always he's shown me books, placing them open on my lap. Art and architecture, Titian and Michelangelo.

I'm still thinking, though, about identity: not English, not Jewish, not Czech, so am I German? You know what, Herz? I'm a European.

Good, Herz says dryly, a person needs a sense of history.

And I'm a Catholic.

Why? Herz snorts.

His eyes are suddenly huge. The room pitches, on the wall is a map: *Tabula Generalis Marchionatus Moraviae, 1790.* Jägerndorf is marked, *Urbes muro cinctae,* a walled city. There! Herz' tobacco-stained finger points. That's where you were born.

I stare drunkenly and for some reason insist: I was born a Catholic.

That's no excuse!

(*Pause*)

You're lucky, you're a Jew.

Herz rocks on his heels, the whisky swirls. His eyes, dark as coffee, reflect light. Look, he says, all roads may once have led to Rome, but in this century there's one major highway that leads to a Polish village just across the border from where you were born, by the name of Ozwiecim, popularly known as Auschwitz.

We're silent for a while after this. The net curtain billows in a breeze catching on the cacti on the windowsill. A smell of soot and smoke comes into the room. It's a hot summer's night.

(*Pause*)

No doubt, says Herz , you've heard from your parents that I tried to kill myself not so long ago. Like your father, or should I say stepfather, I'd learned what had happened to my family.

(Pause)

It was to be on a Friday, this was before my Friday visits to your parents. I went to the studio as usual to finish the last of my commissions, then I locked up. Prometheus Limited, Herz snorts. I was about to chuck the key down a drain, that gave me a shock. I wanted to be in control, everything was supposed to be a carefully considered, rational decision. I took the bus. There were no seats free, that irritated me because I had to stand. Imagine it, you're going to kill yourself, and you're irritated because you can't sit down. I had to tell myself it didn't matter what thoughts passed through my head as I'd already made my decision, I knew exactly what I'd do when I got back to my flat.

I remember, says Herz, the strange impression this building made on me, somehow uncannily familiar, as if where I'd been living already belonged to the past, and I couldn't quite remember. And when I let myself into the flat, something even stranger, the smell of floor polish, the knowledge that someone had been in my flat that day, a human presence, my cleaner, Mrs Parker ... moved me.

I wanted everything to be a rational decision: whether to make up my bed first or take a bath, that was the question. It would be wrong to talk of happiness, but after my bath when I put on clean pyjamas, I suddenly remembered that I'd been a happy child. That was a truly distressing memory.

Should he allow himself the enduring grief of loss, which would be all the memory of past happiness could bring, or stay with his decision, in which case there would no longer be a need to grieve? That now was the question.

Herz got into bed. The photographs of his family face him.

You know who they are, you know what happened to them. I remember as I swallowed the tablets the water in the glass seemed unusually bright. Nothing much happened, so I lit a cigarette. But I put it out when I began to feel drowsy. I didn't want to set the place on fire. I'd given myself three days. No one would miss me until the following Monday. Mrs Parker had forgotten to take her money, which I always left for her in the kitchen. She called the next morning, she had her own key. She let herself in and found me.

You see, I didn't die. Death doesn't matter. If you ever tell anyone about this I'll kill you. *(Pause)* He sighs: Old Mother Time still comes every week with her bag of dust, and she still forgets she's not even to breathe on the Deity of Compassion, let alone wash her in the sink. Sometimes she brings me a pie she's baked.

After this Herz began to paint. These paintings now hang on his walls, washes of colour on board, crude but powerful. One is above the Greek vases: *A river in flood, a solitary swimmer, suggested only by a few ink strokes on a clouded surface, is swept away.*

Another hangs beside 'Melancholia': *A door, as if from a glass house in sunlight, onto a street where faces sweep past, lips drawn back to show dog's teeth, eyes bloodshot, nostrils gaping. This ferocious mob is prevented from entering the yellow-green house, where two small children play, by the menacing but protective shadow cast across the centre of the painting, the figure in silhouette of a man holding an axe.*

The third is above the Goddess of Compassion: *Leaves in a vortex of fire, tree trunks that mark a vast encirclement against the horizon. The eternal separation, everlasting farewell, has already taken place on this curving and desolate plateau where every wind-torn leaf has a human face.*

Who's holding the axe?

My father, says Herz. He's protecting his family from a pogrom. It was a dream.

Herz pours us more whisky. I'm horribly drunk. I like it here, Herz! Books, pictures, music ...

Herz frowns: To continue to be interested, and without desperation, in books and music, and a tolerable life, that's the problem. It's the reconciliation that's criminal: forgetting. Unless one happens to be a member of the So What Club, of which I consider myself the founder – and I invite you to join. In any case, says Herz, God knows what it is that takes the place of conviction with you.

What has Herz just said to me? What has he accused me of? I'm too drunk to understand, but over the years this accusation will haunt me.

We drink a toast: The So What Club!

(Pause)

We'd better take a walk, says Herz, till you sober up.

We go down in the creaking lift and step out of the smelly building. *Die Nacht ist heiter und klar,* says Herz, by Schubert. The night is serene and clear. We go into Paddington Station. There are people sleeping on benches. It's after midnight. An announcement comes over the speakers. Some train or other is about to arrive or depart.

The only reality in life, says Herz, is arrival and departure. He takes a bottle out of his pocket.

You're an alcoholic, Herz!

Whatever else is wrong with me, thank God I'm not an adolescent!

I take the bottle from Herz, take a swig and hand it back. Herz takes a swig. We leave the station and go down dark streets, walking unsteadily, bumping into each other. We come to a bridge over a canal. The water is black, suspended in it a reflection of the moon.

The moon has a somber look, I declaim. I've just read Oscar Wilde's 'Salome', given me by Colin. I climb onto the parapet of the bridge, pull down my trousers and pee into the canal, right onto the moon, into its mouth that breaks into rippling, beautiful fragments

Oh my God, says Herz, your parents! They'll kill me for this! Get down! Pull up your trousers, make yourself respectable *this instant,* and GO HOME!

CHAPTER EIGHTEEN

More of England

Glory be to the father who hath created me! Glory be to the Son who hath redeemed me! Glory be to Holy Ghost who hath sanctified me, Colin chants.

Oh shut up, I hiss at him.

Surely, Colin exclaims, even a lapsed Catholic can appreciate the sheer aesthetic beauty of the mass!

I'm not a lapsed Catholic!

Not *even?*

I've never been religious.

What are you then?

I'm nothing.

NOTHING!

We're on the top deck of a crowded bus, the 131, to Hither Green. I do my best to imitate, if not Colin's flamboyance, at least his scornful indifference to public opinion. I don't allow myself to say what I'm feeling: Don't you *know* the impression you're creating? How can you bear it? Can't you see yourself through other people's eyes?

My point is, I insist, that *one* is nothing. One is a *blank* sheet of paper.

One, dear boy? A *blank* sheet of paper?

Colin is my age. We're in the same class and we are, theoretically, in love. He's such a challenge, I want to kill him. His voice rings out: Why, I'd sooner any day be queer as Pegasus, masturbating in my sad old age! Anything rather than to be tepidly hideously inconceivably *blank!*

People are smiling, I can feel it like a hot breath down my neck. There's sniggering amusement because we're a camp comic turn. This is just one of the many reasons why I can't love Colin, he makes himself and me ridiculous. I can't and I won't be *invisible.* But I want more dignity.

Windsor Road! the conductor calls, to my relief.

This way to the palace! Colin says as we step out into the rain. Now do remember, Adolf...

I'll kill you!

Ach, he doesn't know who he is! Adolf one day, Peterkin the next! Now please bear in mind, we're humble mumbling sort of people here in Hither Green, given to opinions we trust you share. If not, we'll squeeze you like a pimple. If you want to get on with my family, be a humble mumbling sort of person. Shouldn't be too difficult.

Oh do shut up! What mean-looking streets!

The very soul of merrie England. I'm the most exotic thing they've seen around here in years. Ignore the decor, if you can, he says at the garden gate. And be polite to my mother, she's had a breakdown.

The front door opens. Colin's mother is the nearest thing I've seen to a ghost. She's as thin as someone from a concentration camp, her hair's yellow-white, her face ashen. It's as if life has drained out of her except from her frightened, piercing blue eyes. I know what she's thinking as she looks at me: You are evil, you are corrupting my son.

71

Have you prepared us some tea, Mama?

Yes, dear. Some sandwiches.

Thank you, dear. Will you be going to Bletchley's?

Yes, I thought I'd leave the two of you to yourselves.

I'll see you to the bus stop.

Oh, no need for that, Colin

Colin insists, so I'm left alone for a while. How different Colin's relationship with his mother is from the one I have with mine! My mother's fierce, Colin's mother, despite her eyes, is gentle. Pegasus, Colin's dog, rubs against me. He's like a bolster with duck's legs, there are patches of rotting pink skin on him. He follows me, wagging his tail and panting.

Colin's home makes me feel uncomfortably *socially superior.* The carpet, I notice, has stains. The sofa needs upholstering. The colours of everything are muddy, even the roses on the curtains are brown. There's nothing attractive in the house.

If Colin keeps me waiting, I say to Pegasus, I'll cane his bum. Pegasus starts to whine as if he'd understood and just then Colin returns.

Disgusting creature, your dog, Colin!

Colin ignores this and brings in the tea his mother has prepared for us, fish paste sandwiches and jam biscuits. While we eat we discuss Plato's *Symposium,* which Colin has given me to read.

What do you think? He asks me. Is it better to have a platonic friendship?

How can you tell unless you've had both?

How can you have both?

Why not? First one, then the other.

(Pause)

Plato's on the side of the angels, like St Paul.

I don't know what you're talking about, Colin.

(Pause)

I notice a ball of carmine wool with needles stuck through it lying on the sofa. Pretty colour! DON'T unravel it, Peterkin! It's my father's knitting. Only hobby he's got, apart from violence.

Colin hates his father, he's seen him naked. Like a stallion, according to Colin, with his bagpipes hanging out.

Is he physically violent, Colin?

He doesn't actually hit, there's no need. His presence is enough.

Colin winds up the gramophone and puts on a record. The needle screeches across the spinning record, the music swoops and thunders, 'The Ride of the Valkyrie'. Colin shouts: *Für meinen Freund! Für das deutsche Volk!*

Colin's lips purse. When he does this he really is like Oscar Wilde in the portrait by Toulouse Lautrec. He puts on this face because he knows it irritates and fascinates me. His features are elastic, he's going to be an actor. He and Herz are the great influences in my life. I read all the books Colin tells me to read, Gide's *Corydon,* Huxley's *Antic Hay,* and just about all of Wilde. And poetry, Eliot, Blake, Auden, Donne.

Colin is trembling. I know what this means and his question doesn't surprise me. Shall we go up to my room?

Pegasus follows us, panting disgustingly. On the landing Colin points to a door: My parents' bedroom, where I got had. The beginning of my somber joys, as it were.

Colin's room, like Colin, smells of TCP. I don't have much sympathy with Colin's need to clear his pimples by splashing himself with antiseptic. Above Colin's bed hangs a reproduction of Blake's *Glad Day,* joyfully flinging his arms wide, behind him the rising sun. In a bookcase are the collected works of Gerard Manley Hopkins, Blake, Keats, the Bible, Wilde, and Colin's own poetry. I have my own copies of these, on handmade paper with dedications to me in purple ink.

By the time Colin's mother returns from Bletchley's, where she's found the shade of chrome-yellow wool her husband requires, Colin has washed the stains of sin from his sheets and they're drying in front of the gas fire in his room. I say goodbye and hastily leave.

On the top deck of the bus, on the long ride home across London, across the Thames from south to west, I think about Colin, his trembling and his intensity. I can still smell the TCP so I light a cigarette.

CHAPTER NINETEEN

Poor Winston Churchill

Where is that veiling? my mother snaps. What do you think you're here for? Ach, answer the phone!

This summer during the school holiday I'm helping out in the shop. I pick up the receiver: Langée Limited.

Who is it? My mother hisses.

Lady B...

Arrogant bitch! Tell her I'm with a customer.

I'm afraid, I say as mollifyingly as I can for fear she's overheard my mother, Madam Langée has a customer at the moment. Can I help?... The same model, yes. In Somali leopard. Yes, I can make an appointment for you.

Stupid cow! My mother cannot contain her indignation. She stays at Claridge's but doesn't pay my bills.

Friday at two, Lady B...?

I'll see the bitch then, says my mother.

Yes, Madam Langée is free then. Yes, she has Somali leopard. She has all kinds of pelts!

I put down the receiver. My mother races back upstairs to the workroom where her employees, the 'girls', are sewing hats. I'm on duty at the reception desk as my stepfather is out matching samples. I go back to reading ... *as good almost kill a Man as kill a Book; who kills a Man kills a reasonable creature, Gods Image; but hee who destroyes a good Book, kills reason itselfe, kills the Image of God, as it were in the eye.* I've an essay to write for next term: Is Milton ungrammatical? In six hundred words.

My mother comes racing back down the stairs. Where is that blue veiling? Your father's gone wandering off, go to the stockroom and find it for me.

I slip Milton under a copy of *Vogue.* There's a photo in the latest issue of which my mother is very proud: a model poses at the columned entrance of an English country house, she has a wasp waist and she's in a Hardy Amies new look dress. She's wearing one of my mother's hats.

And keep out of the workroom, you distract the girls. The 'girls' (middle-aged) don't quite know what to make of the scenes that occur regularly between their employer and her son.

The stockroom is where our daily scenes take place. We go there to have a coffee and a sandwich and chat without my stepfather interrupting us. I invariably make my mother weep. She comes into the stockroom and things go instantly wrong. You don't know what my life is like, says she, how could you? And your father's come back again with the wrong colours. Do you like those roses? Don't twist them, you'll break them. How many times must I tell you not to go into the workroom? You distract the girls. They waste time. They exploit me.

You exploit them.

You never open your mouth except to hurt me. Don't twist the leaves! Do you know what your father did this morning when Lady A... came! He picked his nose.

My mother's complaints about my stepfather are so constant that I say what strikes me as reasonable and obvious: Why don't you divorce him? My mother bursts into tears. I always knew the day would come when you'd say this to me, she says icily. I only work half days and I want to get away from my mother in tears, so I say: I'm off now.

My mother looks at me with unfriendly eyes. Fortunately we can't argue, a nervous Otto has just opened the door: a customer is downstairs.

I'm going, I repeat. And leave.

CHAPTER TWENTY

Figures on a stage

I'm standing at the window. The flats opposite my room at night remind me of the production of *Faust* I'd seen in Salzburg the previous summer when on holiday with my parents in Austria. In the black cut-out of the building, the windows are stages, lit or dark. In *Faust* Archangels radiating light had hung suspended on high. Below them, in candlelight, had stood Faust and the Devil.

I've become passionate about the theatre. Herz has given me Aeschylus' *Prometheus Bound* and Sophocles' *Oedipus Rex,* and here too I discover windows. I discover I'm a protagonist in a universal drama. My mother enters. Her face, rinsed of make-up, is ashen but alight with friendliness, with something childlike, with that too sweet and dangerous charm that always takes me off my guard. It's after midnight.

As she sits on my bed, a clock in my head measures time: not time passing, but eternity. How pale her lips that are usually brightest red! With the consummate skill of a forceful actress she suddenly flings an all-too-familiar question at me, her voice ringing with accusation: *Do you know what my life has been, do you?*

My life, I want to say, do *you* know about me? I don't, though. I'm trembling.

Night after night my mother tells me the story of her life: How her father had worshipped her and she him, the speed of the cancer, the size of the tumour, how only she knew how to give him the injections of morphine. After a dramatic pause, again the annihilating accusation: *How could you understand?* Did I realise my father had died when I was two? Could I imagine what it was like to be a widow with a child of two? When she married again her brother had gone down on his knees and begged her not to marry a Jew.

The story continues: The Germans march into the Sudetenland, bricks come through our window in Jägerndorf. Jew's whore, they call her. Then to Brünn, where my stepfather was waiting for us. Ja, and then a second time the Germans are here! Did I remember walking with Suzie? How a woman had stopped you to ask if you were Jewish? And in England, with only a pound in her pocket! How hard she has had to work, but *mein Lieber,* she is no fool! Her customers are the cream of society, but half of them are whores!

My mother is not only a heroine, but my heroine. That is why she's a rock in my life, though one on which I'm shipwrecked. She's also the ocean and the storm. I can't bear it so I say to her: *Do you know about my life?*

She spits the word out: Colin!

We sit in silence a while, then: You'll be tired tomorrow, she says, with a sudden shift to tenderness. She offers me her cheek which I kiss, conscious of its softness, of her tired flesh. Now go to sleep ... My mother leaves, the door closes. In the building opposite, no windows are lit.

All the stages are dark. But if I wait, if I stand naked at the window long enough, perhaps somewhere a light will go on, perhaps soon my real life will mysteriously begin.

CHAPTER TWENTY-ONE

A drowning

Along this deserted stretch of the Thames today the trees hang like thunder clouds over the water. I'd follow you to the ends of the earth, dear boy, says Colin, but my feet ache.

We're fishing, or rather I am, with the rod and the tackle I've bought with the money from a wallet I've stolen. Colin has agreed to come with me - fishing, dear boy, really! - because he hopes we'll swim naked.

We're on the trunk of a fallen tree over the water, the branches struggle in the surging current. Colin's shoes are wet, but he can't get them off. He's tied the laces tightly and now his fingers with their badly bitten nails can't undo them. I step cautiously along the wet trunk to Colin, kneel at his feet and undo his laces for him. Colin says to me: *You are so good!* and pulls off his shoes.

His feet are white and flat. The reason they've been killing him, I now see, is because he's put in his arch supports the wrong way round.

No wonder your feet ache, Colin!

Ach Gott ja, says Colin.

Colin has told his mother he loves me. She sat him down in that depressing living-room and read to him from the Bible, that he was not to sit with vain persons or go with dissemblers, and must avoid evil-doers and the congregation of the wicked.

The stormy light turns into a deeper, but luminous darkness as drops of rain begin to fall. Memory, when I can occasionally direct it where I want like the beam of a torch in a cellar, lights that day. Then I imagine I'm rediscovering myself.

Colin, his lanky body among the leaves, his arms spread for balance like skinny wings, makes his way along the tree. He reaches me, then falls on his knees and clasps my legs.

Forgive me! Colin begs.

Get off!

What viciousness prompts me? I bring my knee up into Colin's face. He looks up at me with his cloudy- grey eyes, blood running from his nose, and asks me weirdly: Are you happy?

Were either of us really convinced by this adolescent melodrama of sin, guilt and redemption in which we had cast ourselves? Weren't we mechanical toys, our actions programmed for us by others? Our feelings presumably were our own.

CHAPTER TWENTY-TWO

Making a scene

Above the sofa hangs the painting my parents have just bought. An investment: in an ornate gold frame, it dominates the room and gives the larger flat to which we've moved, now that Omi lives with us, a style distinctive from that of our neighbours, which is exactly what my mother wants. By Frans Wouters (1612-1659): *A Satyr Lusting after a Sleeping Nymph in a Landscape.* The varnished flesh tones remind me of my cricket bat which I've given a venerable appearance of age, if not use, by rubbing it with linseed oil.

My mother is curled up on the sofa. She's in her blue dressing-gown, her back turned to my stepfather and me, heaves because she's sobbing. The sofa is covered in an apple-green brocade. I'm feeling sorry for all the objects recently bought for our new flat: the Meissen bowl decorated with porcelain roses, the Chinese vase turned into a lamp, the little clock with the Cupid, the Louis Quinze chair and the Regency table and the cherry-wood desk will all be broken one day, and that is their destiny.

It makes no difference that my mother imagined her life

would turn out *differently.* Sobs gurgle from her. I feel sorry for my mother. My pity is so paralysing that her refusal to free me from it, to stop weeping and sit up straight and allow me to hang my head and apologise, again fills me with rage. I could kill her.

The dialogue between mother and son that follows with the occasional interjection from the father/stepfather, in which the boy's encounter with the paedophile(s) plays a hidden role in the subtext, goes something like this:

BOY: I want to see a psychiatrist.

FATHER: Ach Gott!

MOTHER: Why?

BOY: I think I need to. I hate women.

MOTHER: If that's how you are you'll have to take a room somewhere on your own.

BOY: Why?

MOTHER: If that's how you are I don't want you living with us.

BOY: Why?

MOTHER: I don't want you living with us.

The father/stepfather, it needs to be said, had been sleeping soundly, or at any rate in whatever sleep veronal had cast him. He had been woken by raised voices he had hoped would soon quieten. As they hadn't, he had felt obliged to get up, slip his feet into slippers, put on a dressing-gown and go to his wife and son/stepson, where he had said firmly as was his habit: Now, you two, make peace. As always, this plea fails. This is a scene with which he's all too familiar; his wife's white and tear-stained face blank of comprehension, of any possibility of communication, as she sobs. The boy, his face contorted with rage, his fingers at the end of stick-like arms flutter with nervous life. The father/stepfather prefers to avoid the boy's mad eyes.

MOTHER: Say something to him.

FATHER: It's his affair.

MOTHER: He hates me! Look at the way he looks at me! He tried to hit me!

BOY: I did not!

MOTHER: What have I done? To deserve this? What?

BOY: Oh, stop it! Please! You bitch! Stop it!

MOTHER: He's hysterical.

FATHER: Now, you two, make peace!

A long silence.

BOY: I'm sorry.

Another silence.

BOY: I said I'm sorry.

MOTHER: Do you realise what my life is like? That your father died, that I was a widow.

BOY: What about me? I suffer too.

MOTHER: How can you say that?

BOY: I'm queer!

A long silence

BOY: Stop looking at me like that!

MOTHER: Do you know what my life is? Do you? DO YOU?

BOY: Oh, shut up! Don't look at me like that!

MOTHER: For your sake I never had more children.

Meanwhile, the Satyr lusts and the Nude sleeps on. The father/stepfather looks pained. Is this where the paedophile(s) come in?

BOY: *(Insists)* I want to see a psychiatrist.

MOTHER: Do you know how much that would cost?

This is not how I imagined my life!

The mother throws herself back onto the sofa where she again curls up in the foetal position. Considerable time passes during which the father/stepfather summons up the courage to look into the boy's eyes. The mother, still in the foetal position, weeps convulsively. The boy moves jerkily across the room to the cherry wood desk. He picks up the Meissen bowl and holds it above his head.

FATHER: Don't break it!

Too late! The boy flings the Meissen bowl to the floor, where it shatters. The father/stepfather sighs: Oh dear! and goes back to bed, first taking another veronal. The mother remains locked in the foetal position. The boy stares wildly, trapped in this room which becomes eternity. Then it happens ... He steps into the bosky landscape above his mother's head, he looses himself in the world of the Satyr and the Nude. Why even imagine it? No, there's no life for him in that idyllic landscape. What should he have done with the money he stole except buy himself a fishing-rod? And stand on the riverbank, dreaming of the one fish he would never catch, his childhood that was over? Why did he steal, except to catch a lost and lyrical world? Why did he fish if not to dream? To climb high into a tree again and listen to the woodpecker's hammering and the pigeon's ruu, ruu, ruu! In fact, Wouters' landscape doesn't allow you to dream. It's a backcloth without depth or mystery. As for actual horizons, those the boy sees daily, the London skylines, they cause him eye-strain. It's hard to bring that cloudy space into focus. Perhaps he needs glasses ... The mother looks up and her eyes focus on the boy with such venom that he recoils.

This meeting of eyes lasts only a second.

As if determined they should remain locked together until dawn, for all time perhaps, the boy again attempts to talk to her about himself, though he dimly senses that silence would be his real strength. As the boy talks, in the puffed white of her face the mother's pale-blue eyes swim, not looking at him, lost rather in some dimly remembered past of her own that later in life will make him look for her in her childhood, her earliest years, in places whose names as yet arouse no curiosity.

CHAPTER TWENTY-THREE

Departure

Herz offered me a painting to hang in my college room. He smiled infuriatingly when he saw me hesitate and said: Yes, if you want it, take it! Hang it in your ivory tower.

My Oxford 'tower' looked out onto a neo-Gothic quadrangle and an *important* tree, with blossoms like full moons. On my wall, Herz's painting: *A door, as if from a glass house in sunlight, onto a street where faces sweep past, lips drawn back to show dog's teeth, eyes bloodshot, nostrils gaping. This ferocious mob is prevented from entering the yellow-green house, where two small children play, by the menacing but protective shadow cast across the centre of the painting, the figure in silhouette of a man holding an axe.* What right did I have to this painting? I'm not a Jew. Why had Herz allowed me to have it? One day, looking out of my window, I was amazed by the sudden existential force of the quadrangle's manicured brilliant green, its explosive brightness. It was as if I were seeing the college lawn for the first time. In a paranoia as luminously bright as the grass I heard a voice say with a finality that was somehow welcome and humorous:

This lawn is more English than you will ever be!

I had a kind of non-existence. If I had an identity forged by something other than a confused and frustrated sexuality I didn't recognise it. There were a variety of destinations stuck on me as if I were a cabin trunk, but the largest label said: NOWHERE. A label that didn't get me far.

I was studying Russian. I planned to take a year off to work on a kibbutz in Israel. My 'moral tutor', an Anglican priest, said to me in deep astonishment: Surely you are not thinking of becoming a convert to Judaism? I must warn you, if you go the college cannot take you back.

My plan came to nothing. I avoided meals in the college hall. The oppressive and inhibiting atmosphere there was an inspiration, as I saw it then, only to loud-mouthed and socially privileged extroverts.

After university my spirits rose. I kicked off with a day's work in Hyde Park, a gesture, picking up paper with a pointed stick. After that, various jobs, waiter, publisher's reader, translator more or less got me by.

I was obsessed with an inner dialogue, with controlling the world I lived in by creating a reality in which I could live. I created fictitious situations and put words in the mouths of fictitious characters: I wrote *plays*. But I controlled the characters I invented no more than I could control myself. I didn't know how to put the people I knew best, those who spoke with *foreign* accent*s,* onto a stage that belonged to the *English*.

I began seeing things out of the corner of my eye, nothing sinister, but I could never turn round fast enough to catch sight of what it was. As for my bowels …The first session with an analyst settled my stomach. After that, we were off! The Old Man, with his thin, serious smile, flowing white hair and elegant, old-fashioned suits, fitted the bill, that's to say, the image: a wise old man.

Does memory lead me into the fabrications of memory? After the war, when I must have expected that I'd now live at home, I found myself again at a boarding school, this time in London. On a Parents' Day to which my parents didn't, perhaps couldn't, come, I hid under a yew, for yew it surely was, I remember the red gelatinous berries. I dug out a handful of wet clay. I squeezed and pressed until it took the form of what I'd never seen: a woman's naked body. A torso and breasts grew from my fingers; between the stems that represent the parted legs I dug with my nails? Was I bringing the clay to life? The making of this image is lifted out of time because I cannot remember when it happened, before or after I myself had been clay, my childhood (or my adult dream of it) abused.

I didn't tell the analyst the clay story, the making of the image of the woman. I failed to recognise until very much later the crippling damage that the 'dubious forger of identity', or more precisely, abuse was giving my life.

After the hour's analysis I would take the long bus ride across London to see my grandmother, who was now in an old people's home. I had put her through sore tests when she came to live with us. One day I locked her in the bathroom. My grandmother pleaded and scolded while I stood on the other side of the door, the key in my hand. I called her a witch. Or rather, as to be understood by her I was forced to speak German, of which my knowledge by then was largely passive, *eine Hexe.* She endured all this and by never telling my mother won my trust.

These bus rides were an Odyssey. I'd daydream, soothed by a sense of possibility, of a future about to begin, though unimaginable. From the top deck of the bus I'd catch a glimpse of a room, perhaps a person in its depths, or the gleam of a mirror. These rooms evoked unclear memories, perhaps obscene. Had I been in these rooms? And what had happened there?

The old people in the Home had all, like my grandmother, been the victims of enforced emigrations, of expulsions from homelands in the conflicts of race and nationality. The nuns spoke German. The building's reverberating silence, the dark but highly polished linoleum in the corridors, the mystery of the closed doors, all reminded me of loneliness and boredom, and somehow also of love. My grandmother's bed was by a window. The light through the tree outside played over her white face, over white hands on a white sheet. Her eyes would look searchingly into mine. What was I up to? All I needed was to be patient, to let my grandmother's stillness enter me, sooner or later she'd say something, remember something, and so would I.

One day she told me about sex, or rather, sex gone wrong. It had been on her wedding night. She laughed, what did she know? In those days no one talked about such things.

The morning after, she had run away, over the frozen fields, through the deep snow, back to her aunt on the farm at Blattendorf.

What did your aunt say, Omi?

Go back! Your duty is to your husband. So she'd walked over the frozen fields back to Daub, as forlorn as the crows wheeling in the sky, back to her husband a year younger than she, to a marriage that had ended twenty-five years later with his death from stomach cancer, though not in 1927 as Franz had written in the *Ahnenpass*, but the following year.

Was it a happy marriage, Omi?

Ach ja!

I made the bus journey to my grandmother weekly throughout that summer and autumn. Then came dark winter afternoons and high winds.

The tree outside the window groans.

My grandmother asks me to call a nun and tell her that the tree outside the window is rotten. It should be cut down before it falls and crushes the house, she knows this because her husband was a forester. The nun strokes my grandmother's cheek and replies: We are all in the hands of God.

The tree casts its shadow into the room. One day my grandmother tells me she'd climbed an apple tree. They'd looked for her everywhere, they'd searched in the house, in the fields. She laughed at the memory, so pleased she'd been with herself for hiding from them high up in the branches, and when she did come down they hadn't punished her though she'd torn her communion dress, though they were strict at Blattendorf.

Her memory becomes an image for me, a folkloric painting burnished by nostalgia. Among the shining apples sits a girl. Above the girl's radiant face, above the ancient tree, the prosperous farm and the green curve of the land and above the old Empire itself, on that particular day the great infinite cup of the porcelain sky is the tenderest blue. It would have been in the 1880s. Bees dip into the fragrant roses that tumble from a trellis that frames a marble bust at the farmhouse gate, on which is inscribed:

Francis Joseph

By the grace of God
Emperor of Austria, King of Hungary

A fierce wind strips the tree of its leaves, the branches toss wildly. I imagine I hear the tree's growling: *I have deep roots.* And my grandmother's stern reply: *Not deep enough!*

CHAPTER TWENTY-FOUR

Father Figures

My mother's possessions, their orbit in my memory, constitute a kind of primal home. The antique furniture, the Meissen plates and porcelain Cupids, even the paintings have long since been scattered in auctions, her clothes given to charity shops. Her jewellery after my stepfather's death she had placed in the safe deposit of a department store, and there it remained until her death.

I remember my stepfather's kindness. How, when I was ten, I had burst into tears at the station where we waited for the train to Wales and, to spare my shame, he took me aside so the other boys shouldn't see me. On one occasion, I was in my twenties, out of the blue he said to me: I have always respected you.

Father figures, fantasies of ...

The scene had the freshness of a Dürer watercolour: the Baltic coast, dunes of white sand in the sun's glare, the green of the shade-giving trees to the water's edge, the blue of sea and sky. I became fascinated by two young fathers, each with a boy of about three. One father and son chased each other, they tumbled in the sand, the man putting out a

94

protective hand in case the child should fall against a stone, and they rolled laughing in each other's arms. The other father could barely hold in his fury during what should pass for *play* with *his* son. He'd push the child over, then pull him up roughly and knock him down again. The boy was bewildered, became excited and shrill, but kept running back to his father. He couldn't help himself, he had to *get close* and fight this rejection. This father suddenly left his son and went to the mothers, who were sunbathing, fondled the breasts of one of the women and began to suck at her nipple. She brushed him away like a fly. Both men's movements were expressive, in the one case graceful, in the other graceless. What I had seen might well have been called the Ballet of the Good Father and the Bad, danced by two men and two children, and made the more intimate by their nakedness.

And then, something else!

I was no longer an adolescent when King George VI died. He was the image of a 'good father' during the war, present everywhere, in newsreels, on the radio. Not aggressive, not even royal. Accessible. Biographers now tell us he was short-tempered and had low self-esteem. The King's lying-in-state took place in Westminster Hall. I put on my black pinstripe trousers and my black jacket and my white shirt with its starched detachable collar and my black tie, in other words my old public school uniform, entirely appropriate for a funeral. I took an umbrella and I joined the long queue to pass by the catafalque. I was humble and proud, I was grateful and British, we'd won the war.

And lastly!

Herz stopped on the steps of the British Museum to take a pill. Then said: Look! He took a cigarette pack from his pocket and sketched a heart on the back. Angina, he explained, each attack results in necrosis, the death of cells. The heart gets wiped out. Herz had blitzed the heart until ink hatching had all but destroyed it, and I'd cried: Stop!

Some years later, I rented a house on a Greek island. The house looked out across the Saronic Gulf to the mainland of the Peloponnese. In the clear morning air the mountains in their craggy detail seemed an arm's length away. On their peaks, as I'd learned from Herz, the beacons had flared with their message: Troy is taken!

I began a letter to Herz.

I wrote that I'd found a *kind of freedom* by leaving England, that I wanted to break with the past, nature would cure me, the Greek sun, the sea - though cure me of what I didn't say. I hadn't yet posted my letter when a letter came from my mother telling me that Herz and been found dead in his flat.

That night I was with friends. I told no one about Herz. We drank wine and smoked pot. Someone played a guitar. We made a bonfire. I began to dance, leaping through the flames as if I wanted to set myself alight. I wanted to celebrate Herz. But as the years go by it becomes harder to hear his voice, to return to that room where Herz rocks on his heels, a glass of that fiery liquor of life in his hand, as he has me listen to music I've never heard before, Mozart's Horn Cancertos perhaps, or a Beethoven quartet, that room that Melancholia surveys and where the porcelain Goddess of Mercy smiles. My stepfather and I might have been closer. Perhaps, when all's said and done, we were.

CHAPTER
TWENTY-FIVE

Bohemian Wilderness (1989)

What truth can there be to memory to which no image is attached, that exists somewhere inside shadows, always round the next corner, formless and never more than a suspicion?

In July 1939 my mother, my stepfather and I had taken the train from Prague to the Hook of Holland for the boat to Harwich. Franz had travelled with us to the border where we had said goodbye. To protect her brother, my mother had insisted he travel in a separate compartment from his Jewish brother-in-law.

This is not to be a *sentimental* return, that's not how I see it. We're tourists, I've insisted, nothing more. Gulls sweep overhead, their cries reminding of coasts Bohemia doesn't have. A swan lifts itself with a heavy beating of wings. We're on Charles Bridge, below us are the dark eddies of the Vltava. The parapets are lined with colossal Baroque statues, saints blackened by pollution.

So, tourists we were! The city is spread around us, the Baroque domes, the Gothic spires, the windows alight in the setting sun. On the horizon are the concrete slabs of the

Communist apartment buildings where Eva, our hostess, had refused to be housed.

We are staying in Josefov in the city centre. Art Nouveau buildings have replaced the medieval ghetto, demolished a hundred years and more ago. Only the cemetery and three synagogues had been left as reminders of the old Jewish world. These in turn owe their wartime survival to a Nazi decision to make them a museum of a vanished people. In a neo-Renaissance house by the Klaus Synagogue is an exhibition dedicated to the Jewish children from Terezín (Theresienstadt) concentration camp. Teachers, artists and others also interned had been allowed to work with the children and they had given them an opportunity to express their feelings, to draw and paint. The children had left a record: the camp hospital, Terezín's guards, the delousing, Terezín at night, Terezín by day; the black wall, the fiery cloud, the empty street. Depressed colours and horrifying detail. Some drawings suggested memories of life before Terezín, a vase with flowers, a room with a bed. Or a house under a blue sky. The dates and names, where known, beside the drawings showed that few of these children had survived. One collage, put together from brown wrapping and newspaper, had one bright colour, a yellow zigzag of lightning striking a girl.

I think of Suzie, or rather, her photograph. Its disappearance has upset me. It had been in the case among the photographs that I had loved to look at when I was a child. Then for decades I lost interest in them, my mother apparently also: the case was stored and for years forgotten. Was it because its contents were reminders too lethally sentimental? No, life made other demands, that was all. When in her old age my mother became increasingly crippled and confined to her London flat where she had moved after my stepfather had died, she opened the case again; like Aladdin's cave it was full of treasure. I visit and find yet another photograph of herself prominently displayed. There she is, posing self-consciously in profile, a chiffon wrap round her bare shoulders, or in a white blouse, white gloves and white beret, hugging her terrier Struppi. This is the past she wants to remember, a past I feel has little to do with me. Perhaps little of it does. On one of my visits I had found the photograph of Suzie. It wasn't that I *recognised* the dark-haired, dark-eyed, soft and gentle face that gazed out with such seriousness and intelligence, but that I *knew:* Suzie had been my playmate in Brünn. We had left for England a month before the outbreak of war. Suzie's mother had not been able to get the necessary visas. After the war we learned that Suzie and her mother (what happened to her father? He was never mentioned) had been sent to Terezín: there her mother had hanged herself and Suzie had died. Recently I asked my mother for the photograph. She is losing her memory and I am forgetful; she says she gave it to me. *Where is the photograph?*

CHAPTER
TWENTY-SIX

Collecting the past

Above the Art Nouveau portico, an emaciated Atlas holds the world on his shoulders. Another sculpted giant clambers the façade to the windows of Eva's state-owned flat. Fortunately the flat is spacious as Eva throws nothing away. Old hats, necklaces, masks, puppets, model stage sets, feathers, bottles, pine cones and bones from Aegean beaches, souvenirs all. There is nothing to regret, she insists, I collect the past.

With her flaxen hair and blue eyes Eva has the look of a cheerful Dürer Madonna, perhaps a genetic inheritance from a Sudeten German grandmother. She tell us about the men in her life, all of them crazy and two of them *alkoholiker*

We are at the window, drinking wine. Below, at the building's entrance, the roof of our car gleams white. It's to take us, I joke, to the other side of the moon, that's to say, two hundred miles east to my hometown, Jägerndorf. We left Prague early the next morning. The landscape became a wasteland of earth mounds and water-filled craters, with isolated houses. After an hour or so we came to an expanse of turbulent water, the confluence of two rivers, where the dark waters of the Vltava meet the Elbe, the colour of clay. The road forked. The turning we took turned out to be a dirt track used by the Forestry Commission. Soon we are driving through forest only penetrated here and there by rays of misty sunlight.

My wife is driving. What shall I do, she asks.

Drive on, I say.

Too late I understand her question.

What follows is my fault. We have just hit a rock. In the rear-view mirror I saw an ominous black spill, petrol leaking, drop by drop like the beat of a metronome, making a stinking puddle out of hopes, more precisely, out of *expectations* I never knew I had. This journey into the mythic past is proving exhausting. I've lost my childhood again: now we'll *never* get to Jägerndorf.

Skandal, says Eva. No one has ever before made such a scene as I am now making. My wife says nothing, nor do my children. I inspect the damage. Wood pigeons call in the distance, ruu ruu! Then sharp and loud, the hammering of a woodpecker. Above me, infinite blue. I am in Bohemia, but stranded. Eva spreads her fingers: Ten minutes, drive on. The dial on the patrol gauge is plummeting. The light falls onto the road, but the sky has flown out of sight. Then a ragged wing of blue appears, then again the trees close in. Then into the open to fields lit by the evening sun. A tractor moves slowly across the horizon.

The road ends at a farmhouse. A woman comes to the gate, Eva talks to her. The woman opens the gate , we drive into the yard. Leave the car here, says Eva, the woman's son is driving the tractor, when he comes back he'll do what he can.

Now we walk to Eva's cottage.

Around us there is stillness broken only by birdcalls and our soft steps on last autumn's leaves, but I am in some faraway and weeping world of my own. I'd told myself this journey was to be like any other, I'd made it very clear that I was going *back* because I was curious, not because I was *emotionally* driven. I was in turmoil. Not only the petrol tank had been pierced, but my defences.

Mein Haus, said Eva, as we come to a whitewashed house built against an outcrop of rock. The valley in the evening light needed only a lion, a serpent and a lamb to resemble an old print of the Garden of Eden.

That hot evening we sat in the garden. The darkening sky, in which a solitary star now hangs, inundates the land, and in this watery dusk an animal calls. The world is calm even though there is murder in the meadow, in the forest. Eva brings more wine from the cellar cut into the sandstone rock and plays us her favourite cassette and now it is the deer and the antelope that roam in the Bohemian wilderness.

Her mother, Eva now tells us, was a relic of the old bourgeois society, helpless but tyrannical, you could feel sorry! A type extinct under Communism. They had never got on well. Eva had wanted a reconciliation, that was why she had nursed her mother in the last months of her life here in the cottage, it had been bought with her mother's savings, ach, that had been like taking an egg from an eagle. Only last year she had scattered her ashes in the valley. It had been difficult during those final months, Eva lamented, because unfortunately she had a terrible allergy to her mother.

When the time comes, will I overcome *my* allergy?

Eva gave us her bed for the night, a huge circular affair that stood in the centre of the low-ceilinged room. Over it an electric heater hangs dangerously, making me wonder why Eva isn't herself already ash.

I hadn't recovered from the exhibition I'd made of myself with my loss of self-control, my hysteria, the wine had helped only a little. The room was stifling and the bed spun. I had a disturbing dream and woke in the night, unsettled by my quest, certain that what I was looking for, or in danger of looking for, was absurd. I was completely unsettled. In the morning I saw that in the night I had written in my notebook: *anxiety - fear of disappointment.*

We left early the next morning. The farmer had welded the damaged tank. Ten dollars, Eva insisted, was enough. Communism suits him very well, he has all he needs, enough to buy his beer and sausages.

The mist had cleared from the fields, soon the sky was a hard blue. I was driving. For this stage of the journey you must, said my wife. We planned to be in Jägerndorf, or Krnov as it now was, that evening. By late afternoon we were already in the Moravian Highlands, in the Altvatergebiet, about which I had heard so much from my mother. This low, forested mountain range on the border with Germany had been part of the Sudetenland. Like all places in these regions it now bore a Czech name, Jeseníky. The air was cooler. Sunlight fell through the tall trees. We had arrived at the small spa of Karlova Studánka, or as it was in my mother's day, Karlsbrunn, where in 1932 my mother and father had married.

We stopped by the Hubertusdum, a dilapidated wooden building. Could this have been the once-upon-a- time 'very

smart hotel' where my parents had their wedding
reception? Among the trees were a dozen or so elegant,
neo-classical clapboard buildings. There was no one about.
It felt as if the spa had fallen asleep and not yet woken to
the Communist state in which it existed, as if a hand had
turned a dimmer switch to lower the bright façades to a
duller white, and if turned in the opposite direction the
faded buildings would again shine with the spic-and-span
smartness of a fashionable resort of half a century ago.

Higher up was a larger building. Windows were open,
bedding hung out. Could *this* be where my parents had their
wedding reception? The building was now a sanatorium.
Karlova Studánka, I knew, was not for foreign tourists, but
for workers and schoolchildren sent here by the state.

We walked under the trees on the carpet of pine
needles. Nearby a torrent fell from high rocks. Then we saw
the chapel. Fallen branches lay across the path to the half-
open metal door where a notice informed: State Monument
of Cultural Interest. A photograph shows my parents in this
chapel. A back view, taken from the door: the chapel
appears empty but for the two attentive figures at the altar,
this strange impression at least conveys the intimacy and
privacy of the moment to the extent that one can tell from a
photograph of two people with their backs to the camera.
About my mother, or at any rate her back, there is an
untypical repose, every other photograph of the period
shows an extrovert brimming with energy. She wears a
cloche hat, a suit, probably light grey, and high heels.

I had asked more than once: What was my *real* father
like?

Your father was the best-dressed man in Jägerndorf,
says my mother, and the most handsome. His family were

poor, but he looked like a baron, people mistook him for the director of the bank where he worked and, said my mother, I will now tell you as you are old enough to know: the director's wife was his mistress. The affair began when he was only nineteen and it lasted fifteen years until I took him from her. She asked me if she could have him once a year on holiday and I said *NEIN!* So she ripped the sleeves off my dress!

The bank collapsed in the Depression and my father lost his job. He became obsessed with the fear of losing the sight of his good eye and becoming forever unemployable. This was when his habit of cracking his knuckles began that so got on my mother's nerves. He got ill, tonsillitis led to septicaemia. His face became swollen and hideous. He told my mother not to bring me to the hospital because I would be frightened. Within a week he was dead. He was thirty-seven.

We went into the chapel. There were faded lilies in a vase on a broken flagstone, but I detected the smell of urine. I thought of my father's nervous habit that had driven my mother to distraction. If he hadn't died, she once told me, she would have divorced him.

I became aware of the sound of splashing water, of the waterfall that they had heard as they stood at the altar. I imagined a starlit, romantic night long ago, their wedding night. I'm two months old already in my mother's womb.

I drove on.

Krnov, now on the border with Poland, was no more than fifty miles away. The road from Studánka descended steeply, soon we were out of the forest. The light was fading rapidly and the landscape was forlorn. Where were the road signs to tell me I was drawing near to my birthplace? Did Krnov exist outside my imagination? I felt a mental shift from excitement to a self-protective resignation. I reminded myself that I'd need to accept whatever I might find, the fear being that I would find nothing at all. This resignation underlay the happiness I had felt all day.

CHAPTER TWENTY-SEVEN

Blue

The phone had rung early, I was still in bed. The explosive sob before she could speak prepared me. In the sudden vertiginous emptiness, the space that opened under me, I heard my mother say: Father has died.

I booked a flight to Switzerland, where my parents now lived, for later that day. I walked with the children to their primary school. All morning it was as if I were afraid to disturb some fragile instrument I carried inside me by making too sudden a movement or taking too sharp a breath; by noon this had given way to excitement. The sensation of blue, cool and pale, became the eye-stabbing light outside the plane's windows. Farewell, England! One kind of waiting had come to an end. Light struck the plane's wing like a solid object. The plane banked, the snow-capped Alps swung diagonally into view.

My mother and stepfather had retired. I didn't visit often. We got on badly. They had rented a ground- floor flat in one of the new buildings that were replacing the old patrician houses, their garden overlooked the lake. I sometimes imagined them in their deckchairs, on a lawn as if cantilevered into the sky, where far below sails moved over sunlit water. On certain days the snow-capped mountains on the horizon can seem to spin and you grow giddy. With binoculars you can scan the distant peaks or look down, past the descending red-tiled roofs, the palms and magnolias, to the sluggish lake where perhaps a swan, swimming past, would fill the binoculars' lens.

My mother was never able to sit for long in a deckchair. She would catch as many of the sun's rays as she needed in a few restless minutes, her nervous flesh never settling into the calm from which, in the last years, my stepfather was irretrievable. She attributed his calm to a wilful capitulation after his first heart attack. You are *not* to move, she would say dramatically. He of course would have shown no inclination to move, his head bent over a crossword rather than raised to scan the world through his binoculars. Too heavy to lift, my mother had said. The sky, the mountains, the lake I liked to imagine came to him anyway, allowing him to settle into a profound, if sleepy stillness. Unable to endure this, my mother would repeat: You're not to move!

He would reply, I'll drive you into town.

A cog railway near their flat took you down to the lakeside in a couple of minutes, or you could walk down the elegant steps under huge dark magnolias. Or you could drive along a steep, winding road. If he found somewhere to park, while my mother shopped my stepfather would stay in the car and gaze at the lake.

I'd taken a train from Zurich Airport to Lugano. My mother was waiting on the platform. She had on a short-sleeved black dress, wore no jewellery, and her face was ashen. Over the years I'd rarely seen her without heavy make-up. The tarmac was melting in the heat. It was still only early afternoon.

Would you like to see him first or eat, she asked.

As the choice was between the morgue and a restaurant, haste for either had seemed inappropriate. I hesitated. My mother answered for me: You need to eat, you're weak from shock.

In the restaurant we sat on the terrace. Under the sunshade it was hot. The geraniums along the wooden balustrade were an intense red. Below us, like a mirror held up and shining into my eyes, lay the lake. I looked at the shimmering water a while, then at my mother.

How are you, I asked.

You can imagine.

But could I? Did I even want to? I could observe, that was all.

Begin with a salad, she suggested. I won't eat. Would you like wine?

I ordered a glass. The cutlery on the white tablecloth reflected the light. Above its glare, my mother's ashen face and black sunken shoulders.

Only two days ago, she tells me, he dreamed he was driving a new car. It had automatic gear shift, he'd always wanted that. He said it was less tiring.

She was anxious that I should eat well. Even so, my appetite shamed me. I was in no hurry for the morgue. I made my glass of wine last as I'd decided it would be unseemly to order a second. When the waiter cleared away my plate and came back with the dessert trolley I was tempted by the chocolate truffle cake, but sighed and shook my head. We ordered coffee.

You should get a haircut.

Yes, I said, I will.

My mother paid and we left.

We walked. I was still carrying my case. The city was undergoing a rapid transformation. The old patrician houses were everywhere being demolished. On the building sites palms still stood in the old gardens, their fronds covered in cement dust. New buildings were springing up, concrete shells that would become apartment houses, angled to give the best possible views over the lake. The city was popular with former refugees – mainly Jews who had fled Nazi tyranny and settled in the Americas and Britain. Some had become the owners of factories, of successful enterprises, in the countries of their adoption. They had chosen Switzerland for their retirement for reasons that included Swiss banking and a desire to be in a German-speaking environment, which Lugano only partly was. Many like my parents received compensation from the German government.

Terrible, said my mother. *Schrecklich!*

She meant, I supposed, the new and noisy cafés that spilled onto the pavements, the predominantly young sitting there, and the heavy traffic. I guided her across the road, holding her arm. My hand brushed against the bonnet of a stationary Mercedes. It was gritty with dust. We came to the hospital gates.

Du wirst sehen, said my mother. But what would I see? It was dusty and airless under the palms. As if to compensate for the leaden atmosphere there was a play of light. Bars of sunshine and shadow moved as if a magic lantern were guiding us along the gravel path to the Chapel of Rest.

Siehst du! The waxy figure was under a muslin drape

that hung from a ceiling rose. I stood beside my mother by the coffin. She clasped her hands and prayed. Then she said, I need air. I turned to leave with her.

Stay, he was your father. I'll wait for you outside.

I decided, before giving *him* my attention, to take in the Chapel. I played for time. Where did the light come from? Was there concealed lighting or did it come from the open door and the two narrow windows shaded by a white blind? A softly humming system was sending chilly air into the Chapel. Outside sunbeams shone through the palms as if onto an enchanted garden. As if unable to tolerate my refusal to look at my father, a fly began to buzz loudly. It had somehow got under the muslin. Was there any point in calling the attendant? My attention again wandered, but the insistent fly had settled on my father's - *stepfather's* - lips.

I wanted there to be an *exchange* between us, that something long known, long felt, should at last be expressed. This in the face of a silence more eloquent than any that had ever come from Otto before.

I was determined not to grieve.

The fly, as if to force a meaning from his death, settled on Otto's nose. Was there anything to remember, anything at all, at this moment?

There is a photograph of me, aged four or five, sitting on Otto's lap. I'm wearing a white shirt, a black tie, I look up at Otto. He looks down at me through dark-rimmed glasses. We're both smiling fondly.

I'd wanted, child that I was, to know his nakedness. He now gave his final answer to that child's curiosity.

In the stillness of the Chapel I felt only release. In any case, desires are what they are; absence of feeling is also a kind of desire. I stepped out into sunlight where my mother was waiting on a bench beneath the palm.

It was still only the middle of the afternoon. What did we do, what did we talk about for the rest of the day? I don't remember. Ah yes, I had my hair cut. And we talked about the Swiss, the swine! She had no sooner come back to the flat, no more than an hour after Otto's death in the hospital, when an official had appeared at the door. He had wanted to put a seal on the desk, on the assumption apparently that it was in their desk that people kept the documents that revealed their wealth. Only intervention by a friend of my mother's had prevented this.

They've already closed the account, my mother said, outraged. They do it the minute a person stops breathing.

Don't you have a joint account?

Don't imagine that makes a difference. The Swiss have always been like this. In the war they turned refugees away at the frontier, *Schweine*, swine!

Were we sitting on the terrace as she told me this, looking out at the lake and the mountains? I don't remember. I only remember that it was hot and the sky was a cloudless blue. Then we were alone in the flat as the light faded.

We went early to bed, perhaps we each wanted to be on our own. I lay down naked on the bed, not because I'd forgotten my pyjamas and was unwilling to wear Otto's, though that was an intimacy I didn't want, but because nakedness just then was a defence: as if in that state I could be free. But free of what? Of the demand to *feel* what I was incapable of feeling?

I looked out of the window. On the patio camellias stood in tubs, the leaves dark and metallic. Trees rose against the sky, but from where I was lying the lake was out of sight. A cypress cut into the moon.

The silence was shattered by a cry of anger, followed by convulsive sobbing. Should I go to her, I wondered.

I felt only numbness in the face of her grief. Would I again hear the all-too-familiar question ringing with accusation: *Do you realise what my life has been?*

What I longed for, I realised, was the cool night air and the sky, its empty spaces, its void. I put on a dressing-gown and stepped onto the terrace. I walked to the garden's edge. The grass prickled under my bare feet. A string of lights, broken here and there by darkness, marked the distant shore of the lake. I imagined I could hear water lapping the stones, and I thought of what was good in my life and had sustained me.

At Otto's funeral I was introduced to the friends of my parents' retirement. My mother had a habit of referring to them by attributes: the Lawyer, the Doctor, the Baroness, the Man from Chile, the Very Polite Englishman. I heard her say to someone of me: He can't cry, it's difficult just like it was for Otto for him to show his feelings.

In fact, my tears flow at the least provocation; poetry, music, novels, theatre and film all can make me weep. I trusted my emotions not at all but was determined not to cry

There was no priest, no one spoke. There was music, Bach, flowers and cremation. My stepfather's conversion to Catholicism had been a bid to protect himself and us, of no avail under Nazi rule and unnecessary once we had come to Britain.

CHAPTER
TWENTY-EIGHT

Homecoming

It was dark when we arrived in my hometown. I stopped to ask a towering figure in black the way to the Moravski Dum Hotel. He put his head through the car window, filling it with alcohol fumes, looked at me with crazed eyes, then withdrew his head and walked away.

The hotel it turned out was just round the corner. The receptionist made no comment, nor did she smile as she looked in my passport which stated my place of birth: Krnov. We left our cases in our rooms and set out for the nearby Town Hall Square. There is a photograph of this square in 1938, on the day of the Nazi takeover, in a 1940 Nazi directory that lists doctors, midwives, lawyers, engineers, mayors, councillors and institutions in the recently annexed Sudetenland. This photograph had conjured sounds for me like a seashell held to the ear, bringing the roar and susurration of a lost world: not the murmuring of the sea but Nazi chanting. White flecks like foam on the crest of waves were in fact hands raised in the Hitler salute to the personage on the swastika-draped Town Hall balcony. I had felt the drama of my early years and a longing for the lost world of my childhood.

A dimly lit arcade led past a timber yard to a smaller square, once Lichtensteinplatz. Not many in Krnov were likely to know it by this name, however, as after the expulsion of almost the entire Sudeten German population the town had been resettled by Slovaks, by Gypsies and by refugees from the Greek Civil War. Lichtensteinplatz was now Revolucni Zámécko Námesti, the 'Castle Square of the Revolution'. We had lived somewhere on this square. A murky light shone from an open basement door of what was evidently a beer hall. This was the Sleski Dum. There was vomit on the steps.

My mother had forgotten our house number. We had lived, she had said, opposite a 'good class' hotel, the Schlessischerhof. Was this the beer hall? Nothing 'opposite', if that meant on the other side of the road, looked familiar in the light of the dim street lamps.

Could 'opposite' mean the other side of the square? We crossed over to the black cut-out of larger houses. No light showed in any window. Evidently people were sitting behind tightly drawn curtains. If I had lived here for the first six years of my life, unless all memory of my earliest years had been erased, surely something in me would have stirred. We went back to the Sleski Dum. What was there to see? A half-open basement door that cast a light onto vomit.

I resigned myself to accepting the otherness, the strangeness of this town, like any other unknown town where one arrives late at night, is surrounded by the unfamiliar and the next morning leaves, taking away nothing but the familiar feeling of having been in the unknown.

We returned to the hotel. On our way to the dining-room, for 'hard currency' guests only, we passed a glass partition. On the other side as if in some kind of ethnic museum, in a miasma of smoke people were drinking beer, among them the unmistakable Rasputin I'd asked for directions.

The dining-room, formerly the refectory, was empty. On the walls were paintings of a dozen luminously pious saints with the emblems of their martyrdom, a wheel, a rack, a griddle. A waiter in tails served us with a distancing formality. A middle-aged couple came in, whispering in German. We exchanged a discreet *Guten Abend.* Perhaps as children they too had lived in this town and like me were on a sentimental journey. Why else would anyone come here?

Would I find anything in this town?

That night I went back with my son. The square was as deserted as before. A murky light still lit the vomit on the Sleski Dum's steps. Something in me insisted though that I was drawing close to my earliest years. The certainty that in the first six years of my life I had been here daily was making me tenacious.

My son said: You're taking this very well!

Oh, I'm not sentimental, I replied.

I hadn't noticed the twin-towered church earlier in the evening. Unlit against a dark sky, if church it still was, it looked derelict. The windows were boarded, the door padlocked. To one side an area was screened by corrugated iron. We peered through a gap. Was this excavation pit all that was left of the cemetery where I had hoped to find my father's grave?

These streets, this town! Somehow held in balance against each other, as we walked back to the hotel, was my acceptance that I would find nothing, that this would be all right too, and the desperate desire to find something here after all.

In the morning Josef would be at the hotel. We were to drive to the Beskids, a mountain range, to meet his family, in other words, *my* family. I didn't want to linger obsessively in the past, but I did want to make some discovery before my never-before-met Czech relatives swept me back into the present.

That night in my monk's cell I woke, as I often do, to anxieties I long ago learned to contemplate until they passed, after which I fall asleep again. While it seemed incredible that after fifty years I was again in Krnov, what was Krnov? My disorientation had to do with time as much as place. Then the wild shriek of fighting cats outside restored everything to the familiar. In the land of the unknown into which I had strayed there was suddenly a sound that belonged to a world I recognised.

When I woke again it was light. The window was open, through it came the acrid smell of lignite dust to remind me that I was in my hometown and that this was in the polluted heart of Central Europe.

CHAPTER
TWENTY-NINE

Where the soil is black

The red flags that hung from buildings looked bleached in the early morning sunlight. The run-down houses and the filthy windows hardly suggested that it was a privilege to live in this once elegant square.

I had become increasingly nervous, dreading Josef's arrival, and had hurried my family back to the Sleski Dum.

The house across the street?

Opposite could surely only mean across the road, *right over there.* I crossed the road. The building *over there* began to *feel* familiar. I then crossed back to the *Sleski Dum* and again looked at the building from there, from *opposite.* The feeling of familiarity went, but I could see that *opposite* was the kind of building where my mother might have chosen to live. Built at the turn of the century, it would have been sufficiently imposing for her clients, among them the wives of the local textile manufacturers and industrialists.

Was it the house *over there?* I again crossed the street and this time walked slowly right to the entrance. The ground-floor windows were too high to look in. An

enamel plaque by the door, from its design probably the
original, suggested that, even if since the days of the Austro-
Hungarian Empire the square had changed its name more
than once, house numbers had remained the same, in this
case: 4. This time not only did the feeling of familiarity
return, but like Alice after she had drunk from the bottle
labelled 'DRINK ME', I felt myself shrink. I suddenly felt
small, smaller than an adult might expect to feel before this
entrance. I felt as if I were a child, as if I were seeing this
doorway from a child's perspective. I took it for granted
that the windows to our flat were to the left of the
entrance and that we had lived on the ground floor. Yes,
the difference of feeling between seeing the building from
across the road, from outside the Sleski Dum, and from
close up was clear. By the entrance I was glimpsing what
for almost six years had been my perspective on entering
and leaving the building where we had lived. There was
always the possibility that I was wrong. That I was outside
the wrong house. But for once intuition seemed grounded
in something discernible, almost palpable, seemed in fact
less intuition than certainty. And yet, I had no visual
memory whatsoever onto which to hang this feeling. There
was no question of saying: Yes, this is the place because this
is the door and these are the windows, of which all these
years I have carried an image. All that had happened was
that I'd had an intensely physical sensation of shrinking and
for a moment feeling I was a small child. I was becoming
tearful.

Josef was probably already waiting at the hotel. I was
regretting my arrangement more than ever. I wanted to
linger in this town. I needed to find my father's grave.

I asked a woman passing by in Russian where the

cemetery was. She smiled and replied in Czech, which I didn't understand, so she led us a short distance to the cemetery gates, which were just beyond the square. I was relieved that I'd been wrong about the excavation pit.

Krnov had for centuries been a German town and this a German cemetery. At the war's end, in the first days of the Liberation, Czechs had taken their revenge and destroyed most of the German graves. However, a mausoleum appeared to have escaped the people's rage, perhaps because it had been too massive to tear down, and ivy now hid the attempts to deface it. We wandered in different directions to look. Most graves had Czech inscriptions, but some were in Russian and a few in Greek. In a shaded corner of the cemetery were a few worn stones sunk deep into the ground. Here the almost illegible inscriptions were in German. Somewhere among these graves should have been those of my father, also called Otto (1896-1935), and of his parents, Alois and Anna.

I tempered my excitement with my fatalism: I would probably find nothing here. At the same time I was still high on the discovery minutes earlier of the mysterious entrance beneath which, for a few extraordinary seconds, I had become a small child.

Shall we ask someone?

Where?

Over there in that building.

The registrar, a middle-aged woman, asked me to be patient and come back in fifteen minutes.

The sky was a cloudless blue. It was a hot summer's day. We again strolled among the graves, again finding nothing.

When we returned the registrar was free to give me her

attention. I gave her the necessary information; name and dates, and she leafed through the *Totenbuch,* the register of burials, a leather-bound tome that had survived two world wars.

Ah, she pointed, here is your father.

Beside my father's name was the grave number, and in the space for his nearest living relative, in the old Sütterlin script in what was perhaps my mother's handwriting: *Hilde Tegel, 4 Lichtensteinplatz.*

The registrar hesitated. I'm sorry, she said, but your father's tombstone was taken away at the end of the war. Things happened then that should not have happened. Please, try and understand.

I already knew what 'taken away' meant. I had the impression from the registrar's concern that she'd prepared other Sudeten Germans who had come in search of a grave, and that she was anxious to avoid scenes.

My father's grave, I said, was beside his parents.

She explained: Their tombstones were also taken away. Their graves were bought by a Czech couple. But your father's grave was still here until 1987. Then it was bought by a young Czech doctor. I will take you there all the same, if you like.

The sun seemed brighter when we stepped outside, the blue of the sky had become more intense. I walked ahead with the registrar on the narrow gravel path past well-tended graves. My wife and son and daughter followed. The registrar now asked me, in good German, those questions I had hoped someone in this country would ask me; about my parents, when had we left Czechoslovakia, and why. I told her about my stepfather. She asked what had happened to his family. I told her his sister had survived, the rest had died. She asked where I now lived and I told her. She then told me that she had worked at the cemetery for fifteen years. She spoke German because she had been forced to work in Germany and had been in Dresden during the fire bombing. She was not from Krnov, but her husband was. She said: Germans who return weep when they discover the grave they are looking for no longer exists. It is very distressing. I regard it as my duty to help them.

Don't worry, I reassured her, I shan't make a scene. I don't even remember my father. This led her to say that people, though they'd kill her if they heard her say it, in her opinion attached too much importance to graves. They ended up feuding over them, tearing out a rose bush someone else had planted too close to *their* grave. It's possible, she continued, that the entire cemetery will be 'liquidated' within the next ten years. She explained: Under Communism there is no cult of the dead.

I didn't mention Lenin. We came to some polished black marble slabs. Here, the registrar told me, my grandparents' and my father's graves had once been. Without really knowing why, I asked my wife to take a photograph of these tombstones. What after all did the young Czech doctor matter to me whose ownership of my father's grave meant that he himself was now buried in it?

What do they do, I asked, with the remains when it becomes a new grave?

They are supposed, she replied, to put anything they find in a paper bag. But they don't. They leave what's there and cover it with a little earth. She described the soil in the cemetery; there were two kinds, in some places it was *gelb* (yellow), *dicht* (dense), *seifig* (soapy) - she must have meant clay - in other places it was *luftig* (airy, porous), *schwarz* (black). Where someone had been buried in clay, then after fifty years there might be bone. If someone was buried in the black soil, then after fifty years there would be nothing left. Here where your father is buried, the soil is black.

With these words, for which I shall always be grateful to her, she gave my quest its meaning. I felt a strong compassion for this stranger, whose absence had been so important a part of my life, even whose bones had now dissolved. For a moment at last I felt something clear about my father and he became real.

CHAPTER THIRTY

Treasure trove

We returned to the house where I had lived: 4 Lichtensteinplatz. The sensation of shrinking was still with me, but already only faint. Was this how quickly the door to that magic land had closed? A young woman leaned out of a window and said something to us in Czech. I replied in Russian and then in German that I'd once lived here, where she was had been our flat and we had left in 1939. She called to several passers-by to act as interpreter and find out what I wanted. They ignored her, perhaps none of them spoke Russian or German. An older man walked by and hesitated long enough to show curiosity. The young woman spoke to him firmly. The man turned to me: *Was wollen Sie?* What do you want? I repeated what I'd told her, which he interpreted. The woman laughed. The man interpreted her reply: She was born in 1952 and for her 1939 was a long time ago. The building, it turned out, was now the *poliklinika* – the town clinic. My wife suggested I should ask if I could look around, perhaps I'd recognise the rooms. This possibility struck me as alarming. To look so closely into the past was beginning to feel dangerous, I preferred to walk away.

But something was still drawing me.

The twin towers of the church, surely those of Herz's cartoon, were not identical as they had seemed at night, but only approximately the same height. The door was no longer padlocked. We went in, but a cast-iron grill barred the way further down the aisle. Dark wood, brass and marble shone, polished and scrubbed, and there were fresh flowers on the altar. I had been in countless similar churches with their floating marble clouds and angels, their ornate carved and painted altars. Here I stepped into a part of my life that until now had been inaccessible. Until I stepped into this church, this church had not existed for me. No memory of it had ever haunted me. But whereas I had initially been prepared to admit the possibility of delusion as I stood outside 4 Lichtensteinplatz, I claimed this church with certainty. I have been here, I kept repeating to myself, I have been here often. It was more than recognition. I had discovered a realm of feeling, as if the feelings I lacked, that belonged to my earliest years, had been left behind here. A door had swung open. There would now be more to discover, more would unfold: the impossible was within my reach.

All that had happened in just an hour or two, the strange sensation of shrinking outside my childhood home, the knowledge that nothing of my father remained, and now the discovery of this church, where as I would learn from my mother on my return to England my father's funeral had taken place, and that after his death she had sometimes walked across the square to sit quietly with me in this church - all this had left me emotionally drained and yet triumphantly happy. I could now leave Krnov.

CHAPTER
THIRTY-ONE

Hats, Daub, more graves.

Josef at a first glance seemed forbidding. In his forties, it wasn't only his greyish-green uniform that suggested police. In fact he was a forester with the Forestry Commission, and that explained the uniform. He told us, in good German, in a deep and sonorous voice that we were to feel relaxed, for the rest of our stay we would be his guests. On our way to the Beskids, as there would be time, we would first stop at certain places that must be of interest to me: Novy Jicín, or Neutitschein as it had once been, had figured often in my mother's and Herz's conversation. Herz would sometimes recite a jingle that referred to the inhabitants of this town's reputation for sharp practice when he wanted to tease my mother for her business acumen:

Neunundneunzig Juden und ein Zigeuner

Machen noch kein Neutitscheiner. . . 'Ninety-nine Jews and one Gypsy still don't amount to one Neutitscheiner.'

Novy Jicín has an elegant square with fine seventeenth and eighteenth century houses, not neglected as in Krnov, but well kept and painted in terracotta and pastel shades. In the small Renaissance castle off the square there is a Museum of Hats, said Josef. Did we want to see it? I said yes.

My mother had hitched a ride on a horse-cart to this town when she was fifteen. She'd sneaked out before sunrise without telling her parents and asked a farmer, Karl Jünger (my mother had remembered the name), to let her ride with him to Neutitschein where he was taking fruit and vegetables to the market. She there persuaded a milliner whose shop was on this square to take her as an apprentice.

My mother had never mentioned Neutitschein's historic connection with hats. It would have been hard not to know about the town's hat factories from which the milliner would have bought felts. These factories had exported hats world-wide, sombreros to Mexico, bowlers to England, and the fez to the Ottoman Empire.

Josef, who knew that my mother had been a milliner, led us through the castle's rooms. I learned that the Neutitscheiners had been making hats since the seventeenth century. One exhibit illustrated the changing fashion in hats through the centuries. Here were hats worn by the famous, and if in Communist Czechoslovakia there were no statues to Masaryk, the country's first president, at least here was his hat.

One display showed an eighteenth century workshop, complete with waxwork male hatter, as hat making had once been man's work. I was astonished to see the same tools of the trade as my mother had used, among them an egg-shaped iron that had fascinated me when I was a child. In our two-room London flat my mother would make up a bed for me at night in her workroom; around me would be the white-lacquered hat blocks she had shaped with these egg irons out of something called 'shpatri'. In the semi-dark these blocks looked like medieval warrior helmets. Even the sewing machine and the kettle had a life of their own.

Daub, now Dub, the childhood home of my mother and Franz, was only a few kilometres away. My mother had talked of long journeys by horse-drawn cart or sled. The deserted road dipped into a hollow and we were soon in the hamlet of Dub, in my mother's day consisting of thirty-two houses, and now hardly more. The road, Josef told us, was the former Kaiserstrasse, the old imperial road, that in the Emperor Franz Josef's alleged words, led from Vienna to *Nowhere*. By mere chance, it had connected Daub to the rest of the world.

It was from here that my mother had hitched a ride on farmer Jünger's cart. My first impression, that this nest of houses lay outside of time, I knew was wrong. Daub had its share of turmoil in two world wars. We stopped at the first house, a one-storey building on a slope of cracked earth and weeds. This brought a man to the door of the house opposite. Who were we? What did we want?

Yes, we were standing outside the old school house. It was now a library but mostly it was closed.

So here I was! In this house my mother and Franz were born! For some reason, what I remembered was that my grandfather had thrown my mother's doll's house out of a window. She was to stop playing with dolls, she was too old. Which window was it? They were all filthy and the rooms were empty. If this was a library, where were the books?

We walked to the back of the house. A beautiful garden, my mother had said. There was no garden now, only a ditch of stagnant water, some stunted trees and wasteland. My mother had reminisced and I had formed images. Fruit trees, the blossoms buzzing with bees. And do you know why my father put the beehives in front of the raspberries? To stop us children picking them! My mother would laugh, seeing no harm in her father's ruse. Yes, so beautiful you can't imagine it! Yes, but I can! My grandmother stands by the beehives, darkly mysterious because a black protective veil hides her face. On it, in my imagination, golden bees swarm. *Don't touch!* And here's my mother, a pretty seven-year-old, squinting into the sunlight. I know this photograph by heart! Franz stands beside her, one arm possessively round her shoulders. The seasons change, snow falls. The children's breath mists the windows. *Come outside and play!* Winters are cold, the snow is deep, but the sun shines and so does the moon and so do the stars. The seasons change, the snowman melts, the first snowdrops appear.

Yes, she'd had a wonderful childhood, few are so lucky! Again her memories form images. Her father carries her out of the house one night, wrapped in a blanket, to look at a comet lighting the sky. If it was Halley's comet she would have been five. She must have been about that age when one day a procession on horseback appeared over the hill and the inhabitants of the thirty-two houses lined the road to watch the cavalry ride past on manoeuvres, at its head Crown Prince Karl, future and last emperor of Austro-Hungary.

Was that distant gleam the river where my mother had led geese to feed on its banks? The sky was dull but hypnotic. Empty fields, a line of trees on a hilltop. This nest of houses, the desolate view and the lone road over the horizon were already enough to explain my mother's lifelong compulsion to live in a metropolis.

The man from the house opposite beckoned to us. He wanted us to meet his widowed sister, here on a visit from Munich. Yes, she remembered my grandfather, she'd gone to the school. People still talked about his daughter, *die wilde Hilde, die nicht tschechisch lernen wollte,* 'wild Hilde who wouldn't learn Czech'.

At his school, to which the German farmers in the neighbourhood sent their children, my grandfather had refused to begin the day with the Czech anthem. He lamented the collapse of the Austro-Hungarian Empire and despised the new republic. This could hardly have encouraged my mother, whose aversion to study was deep, to learn the language. My grandmother, fluent in both Czech and German, saw the need to speak both languages, as would Franz. On this subject, as on most others, her views would have counted for nothing.

The man's name was Kahlich. I wondered why, as ethnic Germans, his family hadn't been expelled at the end of the war. Had he, as a boy, witnessed the expulsions? Or why later his small farm hadn't been taken over by the state. Was it because he had a Czech wife? His sons now ran the farm. As we were driving away I remembered why Kahlich's name had sounded familiar. After the war my mother had sent money to a Kahlich. This was for the upkeep of my grandfather's grave, a rough-hewn granite block surmounted by a bronze stag. Irreligious, the priest had said, but my mother had persevered. It was this Kahlich who had written that someone had stolen the bronze stag.

We drove uphill on the old Kaiserstrasse, past the few

houses, and a moment later we were out of the hamlet of Daub. I glimpsed a motorway in the distance beyond empty fields, but we stayed on the country road. Josef pulled up by a small isolated cemetery. He said: Some of your grandfather's family, but not your grandfather, is buried here.

Why are we so drawn to the places where our ancestors are buried? Is it because to be near their bones reconciles us to our mortality, because they have shown the way into the beyond, into nothingness, where we ourselves will go? Or is it because we become aware of older, earlier selves?

Let's drive on, I said.

CHAPTER
THIRTY-TWO

The Future

The Beskid mountain range rises to 4000 feet. The road
climbed through forest, then on one side the wall of trees
fell away. We could now see the mountains, not naked rock,
not ragged like the Alps, but rounded waves of dark green,
the hunting ground of the males of the generations. Waiting
to welcome us on the steps of a dark, timbered house, the
Jägerhütte, the hunting lodge, were Josef's wife Zdéna and
their teenage sons. Below us, the peaks of the Moravian
highlands rested in the late afternoon haze. It felt like a
homecoming, but it occurred to me that one might feel the
same affinity in places where one had never been before.

Our official reunion, said Josef, with a smile. The stage
had been set in a wood-panelled room. Candles were lit and
a match put to the kindling in the cast-iron stove, though
the sun was still high and the room hot with the summer's
heat.

Josef insisted there should be music, I must select a
record. I chose Janácek's Second String Quartet. Our grins
became fixed as we dutifully listened.

Our family chronicle, Josef said, handing me a book.

He explained, as he opened a bottle of champagne: History in the hands of the state was nothing but a lie, according to his grandfather, who for this reason had kept a record of his own.

Josef translated for us from the handwritten 'chronicle', which was in Czech. We had, it turned out, a great-grandfather in common, Adalbert Bayer (1844-1905), a Sudeten German, owner of a farmstead at Bernatice. Adalbert had two children by his first wife, Irma: Josef's grandfather Anton and my grandmother. Irma died when my grandmother was still an infant and she was raised by her mother's sister married to the owner of the nearby, but far larger estate, which in the family was referred to by its German name of Blattendorf (Czech: Blahutovice). Anton remained with his father as heir to the smaller estate, referred to by its Czech name of Bernatice (German name: Pernartitz).

Silesian Moravia was predominantly German. The owners of estates more usually took German wives. When a year after Irma's death Anton married a Czech woman, Cyrilla, it not only marked him out from his neighbours, but would prove decisive for his descendants. Cyrilla spoke Czech with her young stepson Anton who became fluent in the language and himself married a Czech woman. In 1940 after the annexation of the Sudeten territories, when Anton could have claimed German nationality to his advantage, he courageously chose to identify with the Czechs.

The room was stifling. The cast-iron stove glowed, our faces were flushed. The windows wide open. The sun was already sinking into the trees. We suddenly laughed at the awkward solemnity given to this 'reunion' by the searing intensity of Janácek's quartet. Josef was my second cousin and closest relative. I had, it seemed, several more 'close' Czech relatives to meet. We raised our glasses and drank a toast:

The family!

The hunting-lodge, Josef now told us, was used for entertaining Russian guests, and rented to Americans who paid $500 to hunt boar. However, we'd have it to ourselves for the next few days. Did I want to hunt? I was tempted, but decided not to risk my wife's and children's sure disapproval.

I mentioned a recent article in a British paper that had suggested the playwright Havel might one day be president of the country. Josef shook his head, absurd! There would be slow change, but nothing dramatic. (In fact, four months later Havel was president). The country, Josef explained, needed to be free of its economic ties to the Soviet Union from which it was compelled to import raw materials for its unprofitable heavy industry. Josef wanted to see economic reform in management. He wanted to improve his German as his job involved selling timber to Germany. Another bottle of Bohemian champagne appeared, a cork popped, glasses were filled, and we drank another toast:

Ta the future.

That night I felt as if I were awake in enchanted depths. Happiness as I grew older would surely be easier to achieve. I had come home, but home was myself I knelt on my bed and looked out of the window. A full moon hung over the mountains. How strange that I was so near the town where I was bom, where I had lived the first six years of my life, and where my father lay buried.

134

CHAPTER
THIRTY-THREE

Someone to be feared

Good ideas like Christianity, Karel said with a sigh, once put into practice might work badly, while bad ideas like Communism worked all too well. Not that he was a practising Catholic, but religion interested him. He liked to read the Talmud. He became tearful. It was hard for him to talk about the events of 1939, to this day he could still see the synagogue in Brünn (Brno) in flames. He had lost many Jewish friends during the Nazi occupation. He had memories too painful to relate.

Josef had taken us to see his parents-in-law. Zdéna, their only child, and Josef spent most weekends with them in their house in the small town of Frenstat, where the women cooked while Josef and his sons worked in the garden.

It was a scorching day, but the windows to Karel's book-lined study were shut. He was wearing a woollen scarf and dark glasses to protect his eyes. Beside the Talmud in front of him there was a bottle of Slivovitz, and though it was noon we had already drunk several glasses. You can have no idea, he said, of the isolation we live in, and what your visit means to us.

Karel's father, a Communist, had died in Auschwitz. This hadn't prevented Karel, after the Communist takeover in 1948, from being branded a 'class enemy'. It had been difficult for him to practice his profession as a vet. Fortunately Zdéna had been allowed an education and become a paediatrician. I was saved by the 'little people', Karel said, because they brought me their pets.

Josef wanted Karel's help in translating a passage for us in the 'chronicle' about Franz. I knew that as the war progressed Franz had stopped seeing his Czech relatives, to whom he was close. Contact with them would have been dangerous for them and for him. Franz would also have been suspect because his sister had married a Jew and fled to England. According to the chronicle, which Karel now translated, Franz had risen to become mayor of the Sudeten capital Reichenberg, then become Landrat, District Administrator of the entire Sudeten Territories.

Ein ganz grosses Tier! – that's to say, someone to be feared.

This picture of my uncle was alarmingly different from the image I had formed and cherished. Surely he had never risen to such a powerful position in the Nazi administration?

He must have known, my wife said, what was going on. The transports to the East would have passed through the districts for which he was responsible.

Yes, Karel agreed, Franz would very likely have known about the transports and their human cargo and at the very least speculated about their destination. But the times weren't like people imagine them, you had to live through them to understand. Moreover, if Franz, who would have been highly conspicuous in his position, had

136

been guilty of criminal behaviour he would have been executed.

Why, I wondered, had Franz been interned in Prague? Had he gone there to be with his Czech girlfriend? Had he hoped she would be able to intercede for him? Or had he been sent to Prague already under arrest? Had the information that had come from the Red Cross been accurate: that he had died in the Strahov Stadium on 4 August 1945? In the *Ahnenpass* was the troubling note that said: *Last seen alive in October 1947 in an internment camp near Prague. Nothing more known.*

CHAPTER
THIRTY-FOUR

Illustrations in a child's book

The next day Josef took us on a tour of places the German names of which had often come up in my parents' conversation and still had about them the aura of that long-ago enchanted world of childhood, places where, my mother assured me, I had often been. Karel came with us.

We drove along a country road past fields ablaze with poppies to a small cemetery. A sign read: Polom. I knew what to look for here: an unhewn block of granite. The stag that had once surmounted it had been stolen, no doubt, said Josef, by a soldier of the liberating Red Army. But then I recalled what the registrar had said about German graves in the cemetery in Krnov.

Karel had brought a daffodil. He placed it on my grandfather's grave and wept. Odd, I thought, trying to reconcile the image that had come down to me of my fierce grandfather, now some sixty years dead, and the emotional Karel who had no idea of the personality of the stranger over whose remains he was now praying with clasped hands.

Rooks cawed loudly overhead. Polish pheasants, Josef

joked.

Bölten, now Belotin, was five minutes away. My grandmother had moved there in 1927 after my grandfather's death. In 1945 during the expulsions she had been given a quarter of an hour to leave her home. She had not been expelled from the country and had found refuge with a Czech half-sister. My stepfather had then come to take her back with him to England.

As a child I had clung to memories of Bölten. My mother would comfort me with tales of my grandmother, asking me if I still remembered her. In Bölten my grandmother had stored honey in glazed pots in the room where I slept. In her kitchen were the stuffed birds my grandfather had shot and above the table hung the sticky spiral of flypaper on which flies would alight and furiously buzz as their delicate wings became ever more stuck. These images are still with me.

Bölten lay below the road. I got out of the car and looked down at grey roofs and gardens with sunflowers. What was the point, though, of going down to walk along village lanes looking for the house where my grandmother had lived? The images I retained were illustrations to a myth, itself called memory. Once again, as in Krnov, I resisted. I would find nothing here.

CHAPTER
THIRTY-FIVE

Czech chaos, German order.

Photographs of the dead and the never-met or not-remembered, including my father, had been no substitute for the living and known. Josef had taken us to yet another cemetery, around me now was my extended family of the dead. But then, we all have that! Still, I was beginning to be impressed: burial grounds are a kind of roots. Here lay Anton Bayer (1875-1955), who had chosen Czech nationality rather than German. Karel explained the absence of older graves: there'd been so many wars fought in this part of the world, in the course of which graves had been destroyed. Josef said that wasn't the case, it was just that the cemetery had become overcrowded, so that the dead, his ancestors and mine, were buried here one on top of the other.

Across the road from the cemetery was the Bernatrice farm. It had been taken from Anton Bayer, my grandmother's brother, in the Nazi occupation and only returned to him after Germany's defeat. In 1956, two days after Anton's death, his two sons and heirs were denounced as 'kulaks', forbidden to inherit, and sentenced to two years in prison. The family were expelled from the farm, which became a collective, and forbidden to come within a radius of thirty kilometres. Josef was four at the time.

A rusted tractor stood in the yard, other derelict machinery in the fields. Faces appeared behind soiled net curtains. The farm workers, said Josef scornfully. Did coming here upset him, I asked. No, he accepted as irreversible the collectivisation that had occurred during his childhood.

We drove on. I thought of how these journeys had once been made. Deep snowdrifts in winter would have made the roads all but impassable to the horse-drawn sleds. In summer the cart on which my mother and Franz rode to visit an aunt, a grandparent, a cousin would have trundled its slow way under a blazing sun. Or perhaps brother and sister had walked across the fields and through the woods. That would have been the shortest route.

The road climbed. At the top, where it levelled, we turned off onto a dirt road which became the drive to a large, bleak house overlooking the surrounding countryside.

This was the Blattendorf farm that my mother remembered so fondly. My grandmother was raised here by her aunt. While her brother, who was two years older, grew up in a Czech-speaking household, here German was the language spoken. Unhappy at the collapse of the Austro-Hungarian empire and the subsequent creation of the new Czechoslovak state, by 1940 the family at Blattendorf were Nazi sympathisers. Had they not been, it would have made no difference. In 1945, along with some two and a half million other Sudeten Germans, they were expelled from Czechoslovakia.

Here things had been done, according to my mother,

not as at Bernatice where there was *böhmische Ordnung*, in other words, 'Czech chaos', but in the German way. The farming methods had been the most modern, that went without saying. Here there had been *Tradition und Kultur*. There had been a piano, my mother assured me, as if possession of this raised the Blattendorfers to cultural heights unimaginable at Bernatice. The house, my mother had never tired of telling me, was an *Erbrichterei*. This meant the owner of the property had been granted the hereditary office of magistrate or might have bought the title which by the nineteenth century was up for sale. The *Erbrichterei*, I should know, was the oldest house in the community and its owners the first family. When "Grossi", the ancient matriarch at Blattendorf, came into the room, you curtsied. When she rode by the men doffed their caps. My mother's description of Blattendorf, where she was often taken by my grandmother, had always sounded so grand: the Italianate garden with lilies and roses, the espalier trees on which luscious peaches grew, the sumptuous hospitality, the table laden with food and drink, the porcelain, the silverware and crystal. *Tradition und Kultur!*

My grandmother had been the poor relation at Blattendorf. In Bernartrice, her Czech stepmother Cyrilla had put by her dowry, her dead mother's linen, tableware and jewellery. When my grandmother married she had moved from here to the school-house at Daub.

Country paths, short distances! Nationalism and war would create unbridgeable gulfs! The Blattendorfers, as my German third cousin Erika from Blattendorf would one day tell me, had entertained 'high-ranking German officers' here. After the war my mother had sent food parcels to the

Blattendorfers in Bavaria when they in turn were refugees.

Erika and I had played together as children, not that I remembered. A photograph shows us sitting together in a little cart harnessed to a goat. I met Erika again decades later when she came to stay with my mother in London. Then in her fifties, a few years older then me, she ran a small grocery store in Munich and had never married. After a glass or two of wine she forgot herself sufficiently to reminisce about her wartime childhood at Blattendorf. I listened intrigued while my mother fell stonily silent. Happy days! Gone but not forgotten, her happy childhood! The smart uniforms of the German officers, the handsome men! Her first kiss had been from a German officer. Erika too had talked of "Grossi", the matriarch at Blattendorf, telling an old and well-rehearsed family story, the ride in a gig through the town and the doffed caps. She too had painted an idyllic picture but the German officer had put a sour look on my mother's face. Sensing our reaction, Erika had excitedly reassured us: we could have no idea how well-bred the German officers had been and to this day she found it hard to believe the crimes of which the Germans were accused, those who spoke of Auschwitz should only know how viciously the Czechs had treated the Germans at the end of the war. She herself had never heard a single word said against Jews, then or now. In the embarrassed silence after this statement I had refilled our glasses. Erika, in drunken confusion and beginning to tremble, had then told us of what she had witnessed as a child during the Czech expulsions of the Germans, the beatings, the killings, she had seen human brain splattered against a wall . . .

An elderly couple had come out of the Blattendorf house,

with them a small boy, barefoot and naked but for a vest. While Josef spoke to the man in Czech I spoke to his wife in Russian. The couple, I already knew, were Czechs whose ancestors had emigrated to Russia. They had returned to Czechoslovakia in 1948 and the man was now the manager of the farm which had become a collective. The little boy was their grandson.

The woman began telling me a story, and wept. At first my Russian was inadequate, then I realised she was talking about her mother's death. It had happened during the famine in the Ukraine, her mother had died in her arms. She was telling me of what had occurred half a century ago. Meanwhile Josef was explaining our presence to her husband.

Would we like to come into the house?

Over coffee in the kitchen the farmer told us: the farm was their home, had been for the last thirty years, but it was becoming increasingly difficult to manage. I looked at the bare walls. I had been fascinated as a child by photographs of these same walls with their trophies of the hunt, the row upon row of bleached, antlered skulls. I now imagined these skulls stampeding from this house, in a wild and ghastly flight, as the former human inhabitants had done. All trace of that particular past had long since been wiped out and now on the walls there was only a clock that ticked loudly and a calendar where the dates were crossed off daily. I thought of my grandmother growing up here.

Outside the house, as we were saying goodbye to the farmer and his wife, their grandson ran to pee against a tree. The house stood on a height. Beyond the chestnut trees along the drive, fields sloped down, then rose again in gentle hills to the horizon. All this land still belonged to the farm. The fields were fallow, no animals grazed. There was no sign of farm machinery. Where are the animals, I asked. Over a hundred pigs in the barn, said the farmer. Where are the farm workers, I asked. Where, sighed the farmer.

The little boy was still peeing. Again, when I least expected it, a memory slipped into place. I'd done just that here on this drive, peed against trees. This memory was so startlingly clear that it solved the mystery of the goat cart in which I sit with Erika. Now it all came back, that day the goat had butted me in the stomach, quite gently. I'd shrieked hysterically and have been a little afraid of goats ever since. This had happened here, on this drive, in front of this house.

So Blattendorf was a part of my history too! So now I knew it for a fact, I'd played on this dirt road, I'd been in the rooms of the house, I'd seen the skulls, I'd seen these fields already long ago. In some small way, I belonged here too: this delusion enhanced the moment, the sky became brighter, the scudding clouds fresher, and this because memory had plunged me intensely into the here and now.

I felt, not for the first time on this journey, close to my mother. I remembered that she had talked about a chapel the family had built to commemorate the men from the local community who had died in the First World War, one of whom had been the Blattendorfers' nineteen-year-old son, my mother's favourite cousin and heir to the estate.

There was a small, rather ugly red-brick chapel along the drive. The door was locked. I peered through a filthy window. Dead leaves had blown in under the door. I remembered my mother saying the family had commissioned a carved Madonna, perhaps it had stood on the marble slab that must once have been the altar. Should he look for the key, the farmer asked. I said, no. There were wild flowers, poppies and buttercups, in the uncut grass around the chapel. I picked some and later that day laid them between newspaper inside a book. By the time I was back in London they were pressed. I had them framed in a gilded frame and gave them to my mother who hung them by her bed.

CHAPTER THIRTY-SIX

Cousins

Let me bring them together, these second cousins and third cousins. I'm meeting them for the first time, let me put them round a table on which there's a cut-crystal bowl full of fruit, plates of rye bread and salami, bottles of beer and a bottle of Slivovitz, and above the table a large painting of a nude reading a book. On a shelf are books on Russian architecture and a volume on Henry Moore. We are in the house of Josef's elder brother. Pavel is the director of a major industrial enterprise where he has found jobs for his wife, his son and his daughter-in-law. He's managed this, he tells us, without becoming a party member. I speak Russian with them as this is the language we have in common, this surprises and pleases Pavel and his wife Kamila. They are off to Moscow shortly and as they're apprehensive about not getting enough to eat in Gorbachev's Russia they're taking plenty of salami.

Unlike Josef, Pavel has no sentimental desire for a bond with that branch of the family in the West that I represent. There are no reverential questions about my mother who Josef insists is now 'the head of the family' because of her great age. Either the slivovitz has made my

Russian more fluent or completely incomprehensible, impossible to tell which from the grinning faces around me.

And now, on our last day, we're at Petr's, another second cousin. He lives in a village outside the ancient city of Olomouc in Central Moravia, and we've stopped here for lunch before driving back to Prague for the night, then Cologne for a night, then on to Holland, the ferry and Britain. This meal too is a celebration. *I am a kulak's daughter!* With these words Petr's mother Magda begins her story as we stand round the table with our glasses raised. She is Josef's aunt and my mother's much younger first cousin and she startles me by her resemblance to my mother. I've never seen that nose, my mother's finest feature, on anyone else before. Magda's dominant personality soon suggests another resemblance. Her son Petr, with whom I instantly identify, wears an idiotic grin as he listens to his mother.

There's pork and dumplings, and of course there's slivovitz and Moravian wine on the table, though I mustn't overdo it. I'll be driving. We drink a toast. Once again:

The family!

Magda, prompted by me, continues her story. Under Communism, she says vehemently, she has been denied everything. That in the war her father had rejected German nationality, that under Nazi occupation he had already once suffered the confiscation of his property, had counted for nothing. The day of his death in 1955, her two brothers, heirs to the Bernatice farm, were arrested and the farm taken from them. To own a plot of land or have bourgeois ancestry was a crime. Her brothers were sentenced to two years in prison as members of the 'criminal bourgeoisie'. She had spent those two years going from one prison to the other to see them.

Magda told her life's story as my mother told hers. Perhaps it too had been told often before, rehearsed and shaped by bitterness. Or was I the listener from the West for whom she had waited for a first telling? When she told me how I reminded her of Franz - and wasn't there something about Petr that reminded me of my dead uncle? - I felt tribal: I belonged. The desire to 'belong' I had always thought of as a desire to delude oneself, a refusal to understand how deeply dispossessed we most of us are. Now my grinning drunken self was saying: I belong. Could I have felt this without the welcome I was everywhere being given? I suddenly had an *identity*. I had gone *back*, to my birthplace, I had come to my father's grave. I had come to people for whom I was family. I had done this in a trajectory that sped past the failures and humiliations of my life like an arrow to its target. As Magda talked about her life I sat back in my chair, a little drunk and still inwardly grinning. I had a rare sense of knowing *who I was*.

Magda's anger increased. Everything, every opportunity had been taken from her. She had been cheated by a regime of criminals. Don't complain so, Mother! Petr said cheerfully. Born after the war and under Communist rule, with no experience of the Nazi occupation or life outside Communism, like Josef he looked forward to the slow change and liberalisation from which he would benefit.

Josef, smiling, though not with the genial imbecility of Petr, turned to me and told me that in the old house at Bernatrice there was a cupboard on which he'd carved his initials when he was a little boy. Whenever he drove past the farm, which he now did often as the thirty kilometre restriction had been removed, he thought of that cupboard. It could well have been used for firewood, but for him that cupboard with his initials on it would always exist.

We each have those cupboards, I said.

The room was hot, the sun shone in. Petr owns this house. It's spacious, well built. He built it himself. At last, we all wander out into the garden... flowerbeds, dahlias... rows of onions, beans ... I'm drunk or ecstatic, one or the other, both are risky... Please, closer together now! No need to tell you to smile, Petr!

Photographs, photographs...

We can't delay at Petr's a moment longer...

Goodbye, goodbye!

Petr, his wife, his daughters and Magda, stand in the street and wave. Josef and his family drive back home in one direction, we in another.

I felt as if I had conquered time.

Three days later we were on the overnight ferry from Vlissingen to Ramsgate. I lay awake in the pitch-dark of the hot and airless cabin which the four of us were sharing. I couldn't sleep. There was the hum of the ship's engine. I tried to fill the dark with light, that's to say the light of memories, but no light, no memory of the journey I had just made came, only a sensation of the solid dark closing in and crushing me. I got up from my bunk, hit my head against something, lost all sense of the space around me, which became vast. In my panic I couldn't find the light switch. I groped and found a handle, opened the cabin door and escaped.

On deck I felt better. Stars hung low in the sky. Black waves rolled like the Beskid mountains. The ship glided smoothly. After a while I went back to the cabin and lay down again.

I fell asleep and had a dream. I had sailed to an island and climbed a cliff path to a familiar house, in fact, a house on a Greek island where for many years we had spent our summers, which somehow was confused with the church at Krnov. In my dream only the roof of the house was visible beneath rampant vegetation. Out of this jungle rose a single blue flower. I felt I ought to continue along the steep path that had brought me this far, past this house, and climb higher to scale the mountain above. But I could see no way forward. I would have to take the dangerous cliff path back down to the sea.

CHAPTER
THIRTY-SEVEN

Diary

About German unification my mother says: *Now comes the unification. The English will see the Germans will gobble them up if they don't pull their socks up.*

About the Thames Water Company:*There is no water, the street is flooded. I hate this country. If I could think where we could all go I would take us all and we would all live somewhere else.*

About Mrs McGonagle taking a holiday: *What has she got to do in Ireland? With all those troubles? With me she gets the same pay as if she would work. She is dangerous, she brings me flowers.*

I was listening to Schumann on the radio while noting my mother's sayings, *Sehnsucht nach der Waldgegend* (Yearning for the woodlands). What amuses me about these melancholy songs of the yearning to wander afar, to distant mountains and lonely shores, etc., is that Schumann always felt great anxiety before a journey and needed to drink heavily. Schumann was interrupted by Mrs McGonagle's phone call. I'm with your mother, she announces, she's very depressed. Can you come round immediately? Mrs McGonagle also says pointedly that she looked after her own ailing mother, her voice drops to a whisper, to the day she died. The implication is clear: Mrs McGonagle is tired of the responsibility she feels should be mine.

You will come, won't you?

Perhaps, I replied and hung up. What *now*? Should I go?

I'VE BEEN! She seemed far from depressed, what did we talk about? Money. She tells me she promised Otto before he died (a lie!) never to give me 'power of eternity'. I reassured her. I had power of attorney but I would not abuse it. I was relieved when she sighed and said: I am forgetting everything, you must take control.

Compassion. *The difficulty, as an adolescent, of feeling compassion. The demand for it was too violent. The vacuum this creates fills with rage or indifference.*

Safety. *The precarious clinging to a notion of identity that memories, probably fictitious, uphold, like a climber clinging to the crumbling face of a cliff in the delusion that by gripping he can prevent the cliff face from crumbling.*

About herself: *Ich hab' so schreckliche Träume von alles was ich erlebt habe, aber im Traum ist es noch schrecklicher.* 'I have such terrible dreams of all I have lived through, but in my dreams it is even more terrible'. - Then we have coffee and cake and by the time I leave she seems content. I step onto the street and look up and yes, she's at the window and when she sees me she waves. I walk away but turn every few yards to wave back. My heart is wrenched because this is the longest goodbye.

A myth: the golden beginning, in which I believed because of the Sudeten stories my mother told me, and now that she is old and frail I want to believe in a golden end. I wish a golden end for her, I'd give it to her, if I knew how; against this dream is the reality, not the chronic pain from osteoporosis, but her inability to focus on anything other than her pain, whether from the osteoporosis or another of her many conditions, also her overwhelming self-pity that makes it impossible for her to find any blessing or good in her life, so that she laments, 'why have I only inherited the bad from my mother.' Her tears and complaints are resented and Mrs McGonagle says she is 'putting it on'. The golden end for a while seemed within reach because she had been prescribed anti-depressants. Now she refuses to take them.

Mrs McGonagle tells me my mother saw Otto in her bedroom last night. She woke up hungry and he told her there was ham in the kitchen, so she got up to look - he was right. Mrs M and I chat in the kitchen, because in the living-room the television is on full volume, soon the people upstairs will be banging on the ceiling. Mother is watching *Top of the Pops,* standing shakily, staring at the screen and muttering, terrible, terrible .... I made her sit but she continued to watch, leaning forward for fear she might miss something, as if she longed to plunge into the screen and take part in that frenetic activity of the young, and all the time went on muttering, terrible, terrible! ... I couldn't bear it and turned down the sound, then suggested we try another channel and flicked to the news, starving children with flies on their gummy eyes, racked bodies, distended bellies. Mother began to cry, muttering, terrible, terrible ... Suddenly she hardened: Enough! I cannot think only of the world, now I must think of myself! Turn off the television!

Sunday evening, Mother has just phoned. She needs to see me, I'm to drive over instantly. She can't say over the phone what the matter is. I said I couldn't. As usual when I don't fall in with her plans she became hysterical and aggressive, saying I will have to take the consequences . . . This is hardly the first time she's threatened to kill herself. I'm so weary of this lifelong bullying that I said I would take the consequences... A second phone call, she's depressed, refuses to say why and wants a visit INSTANTLY...

I SHOULDN'T HAVE GONE. She says I took advantage of her age to make her sign over her property to me, repeats that Otto had made her promise before he died never to give me 'power of eternity' – well, she has that over me! Again I reassure her. This all has left me excitable and nervous . . . It's 2 a.m., I'm at my desk, I can't sleep ... I'm taking three sleeping pills. I want a few hours of OBLITERATION.

Ovarian cancer. Mrs M took her to the hospital ten days ago for an examination. While there she developed severe stomach pains and they kept her for emergency surgery. Before the operation she called me Peterle, she last did that before we came to Britain. The cancer has spread throughout. The consultant has said it is a matter of months, or even weeks.

Mother thinks she's been in hospital for only one day. Perhaps she lost consciousness and was brought in, she suggests and asks me: Did she have a stroke? Is amazed when I tell her she's been in the hospital for three weeks and cannot remember that she has had an operation. Is it serious, what I've got, she asks, but doesn't seem to relate her stomach pains to why she's in hospital. - I do not think she really wants to know what she has, I say to the nurse, Farah G, a kind, serious and intelligent young woman, who agrees with me.

She likes the ward, back alone in her flat could be boring, here it's lively and interesting, she also likes it because it's a mixed ward. Where else, a gay visitor jokes, would she be next to a man in bed at her age? She grins, but may not have heard this remark accurately. The constantly changing staff rarely have time to read the patients' notes, so they don't know the reason she can't walk is because she could hardly walk before the operation because of her osteoporosis, or that even though she is healing well she has terminal cancer.

A nurse had pinned an I AM 90 brooch from her birthday card to her nightdress. If a year ago she could have seen herself like this she would have been outraged at the indignity. I congratulated her. What, she says, me ninety! There was commotion outside, my wife and I went to the window to look. In the courtyard there was a fire engine, a few people were leaving the opposite wing of the hospital. There seems to be a fire, I said to Mother. *Ach Gott*, she said, the things the English do!

She had a bad night, the staff nurse warned us. She was lying flat on her back, ashen-faced, looking fierce and prophetic, I doubt if she knew who I was. Or perhaps she did as she then said, *Du hilfst mir, woraus ich mir gar nichts mache.* I let go of her hand, crushed by this remark: 'though you are helping me, this means absolutely nothing to me'. She seemed blind but all-seeing. My wife and I sat by her bed and listened to her mumbling. In a strangely grave voice she spoke to someone who must at that moment have stood before her illumined by memory: *Ich trage dein Kind,* I am carrying your child. To whom could she be saying this but to my father? I knew she was two month's pregnant with me when she married him. Her tone was neither a threat, a plea nor an accusation, but a tone I have rarely, if ever, heard from her: uncannily calm, a statement of a fact that it was essential to profoundly consider. Or perhaps it was after all a question: I am carrying your child. What is to be done about this pregnancy? Will you marry me? I felt, as I leaned over her to catch every whisper from her lips, as if I were looking into the clarity of the past as if through a tunnel into daylight, to something that at that moment was utterly intimate and vivid to her, on which her fate and mine depended. It was as if the mists of time had parted, a somewhat trite cinematic image, yielding to a flashback that was nonetheless spine-chilling and gripping. In her mumbling she next repeated one phrase several times: *Eine anständige Frau trinkt Bier, sie trinkt kein Wein,* 'a decent woman drinks beer, she doesn't drink wine'. Do I hear the voice of her parents here? Her puritanical mother, her

157

disapproving father, telling a rebellious, but really still intimidated girl, that she has been wild and unruly? After a while, as I strain to hear, she says in a strange, imperious and hoarse whisper: *Was man nicht hat kann man nicht haben,* 'What you don't have you can't have'. Yes, I could recognise her iron will in that, and her coldness too. Rightly or wrongly I took it as meant for me: I had demanded too much from her all my life. As if to make sure I hadn't misunderstood, finally she says: *Mein Popo ist voll von deinem Kram,*

'My bottom is full of your junk'.

She has been moved to a single room and is on a morphine pump. While she sleeps I look out of the window at the inner courtyard of the hospital, a state-of-the-art flagship of the Health Service, recently built and much criticised for the enormous cost. The view from her window is onto a thirty-foot mobile that hangs in the vast inner courtyard.

When she wakes we chat a little. Her eyes close.

Are you sleepy, I ask.

Slowly my question sinks in. Without opening her eyes she says indignantly, Don't you try telling me I'm sleepy.

February sunshine. For Mother the past has become the present. For me, so often in search of the past, of just this transcendence, this epiphany, there's an eerie satisfaction in finding myself with her at the high altitude of this morphine plateau.

Ist die Mutter aufgeregt? she asks me. 'Is mother very upset?'

She means her own mother. Mother, I say to her, granny died forty years ago.

Ach, siehst du... ich bin verblödet. 'You see... I've turned simple-minded'.

Do you remember your mother, I ask her, when you were a little girl?

She replies, suspicious and indignant, Why do you ask?

I realised with alarm what my question was about. The thought behind it: Now that you are dying do you think of your mother, my grandmother, and does the manner of her dying bring you strength and comfort?

I had to cover up: she is not yet prepared to admit that now she too is dying. In confusion I replied: Because you talk about her all the time. This seemed to satisfy Mother because she then said quietly: I think about her all the time (or perhaps she said this in German).

Mrs McGonagle sat with Mother this afternoon. When I arrived Mother had just dozed off. Mrs McGonagle told me Mother had said how fortunate she was to be in this lovely room which I'd had specially built for her as an extension to my house. What does Mother make of the giant metallic blue and green wings of the mobile outside the window, I wonder. In her morphine dream, perhaps they are the fruit trees in the orchard at Daub.

That face in sleep! If I had the courage I'd photograph her. I'd wanted to stay longer, but after two hours... I am sad Mother's life is nearly over, quite a heroic life... I understand her best when I see the child in her, something impossible while I was young: in a sense I 'found' her in Daub, that nest of thirty houses where she spent her childhood. I saw the child.

159

The staff nurse tells me that what we are seeing, the spasms every ten minutes or so, and lasting about a minute, will not be experienced as pain if the face is relaxed, and on Wednesday I had in fact noticed that her face was relaxed and didn't suggest that she was in severe pain. This time, during a spasm, I asked her if she was in pain. Not at the moment, she managed to reply before sinking back into a morphine sleep.

Her naked shoulders, skeletal, pitiful, fine-boned and beautiful. On this surgical ward people are meant to recover and be discharged, the nurses don't have time to look after a geriatric and dying patient. They have not given Mother a clean nightdress but left her naked under a blanket.

Last night, a phone call from the hospital. Today, as planned, Mother will be moved to a palliative care unit, in other words, a hospice. Everyone wishes *me* good luck, even the nurses. As if I'm the one who needs luck while my mother is slowly dying! I dreamed that I comforted my dearly loved and crippled brother. Telling my wife this dream I burst into tears and found the words that I suppose define my relationship with my mother: An unrequited love, she could not give me what I wanted and I could not give her what she wanted.

Mother asks where she is. The move to the hospice has confused and distressed her. I should have gone with her in the ambulance, but had decided instead to come later, allowing her a couple of hours to settle in. I told her she was in a convalescent home. Did I need to lie? She let me look deep into her eyes and surely she was telling me what she was not putting into words: *Don't leave me. Do you realise what is happening? Will I see you again?*

I did leave exhausted and went home. A nurse had told me you can never predict, it can happen at any moment, not only with her, with anyone. You can be at the bedside day and night and only leave for a couple of minutes to go to the lavatory, and that's when it happens. We were with her yesterday afternoon, then my wife and son left. My daughter and I stayed. She was in a deep sleep throughout. She died at 1.15 a.m.

My mother was a dramatic teller of the tale of her life, the flight from Nazi persecution, the refugee years in England, the need to support her family and how she'd succeeded. But the dozen people at the funeral know this. She hadn't found it easy to be happy, I said. She'd clung to what had been tragic or painful in her life. Should I have said this? My funeral oration was meant to be a tribute

Even so, I said, she'd had a happy childhood. I spoke about Daub, where the little girl had been known as'Hilde, the wild one' – this produced a guffaw from an old friend. I told how one night her father had carried her from the house to see Halley's Comet, she would have been five. How one day she'd stood with her parents and her brother Franz at the roadside and along with the inhabitants of the hamlet of Daub watched the future and last Emperor of Austro-Hungary ride by.

I said that memories of her childhood had sustained her, they had made her happy and I hoped, in fact I knew, that she had drawn comfort from them, above all from memories of her parents, especially her mother, towards the end.

I had, with my experience of radio drama, planned the timing of the readings and the music to the second, printed this out and as instructed, given it with a tape cassette to the organist who as well as playing the organ operated the tape deck hidden behind a screen. I bore in mind what a friend who had recently lost his mother had told me: Enjoy the funeral, if you can.

My wife and I had played the last movement of *Eine Kleine Nachtmusik* countless times before settling on the precise moment for committal, at 3 minutes 56 seconds into the track. It was really too theatrical, I felt almost embarrassed at our perfect timing and thought of the Commendatore in *Don Giovanni* as the Don is dragged into hellfire, as the coffin with my little mother slid out of sight.

CHAPTER THIRTY-EIGHT

Power of eternity

4 March. Smoke is still pouring from the incinerator, we've been burning the leaves... the sparks fly into the starry, frosty night. I felt as if we were on a ship travelling through a starlit universe. I was mesmerised

...I've had kind letters from friends who have lost mothers, they all somehow are counterweights on the scales against the two dreadful words that arose in me, moments after my mother died... words I finally dared tell my wife who laughed astounded, but understood when I said they had come unbidden into my mind ... *Good riddance!* I try to tell myself, but have no way of knowing since the dreadful words rose in me unbidden, whether I was saying goodbye to the pain and suffering of this life or good riddance to my poor old mother.

2 April. I look at photographs of her, I feel nothing, or rather, it's a veiled feeling. Something hidden from me? What am I expecting to happen? Last night I dreamed she'd turned into an owl, this happened on the landing outside her flat. I led her by a wing to an open window, the night sky

outside was a wonderful Titian blue. I told her to fly. Unfortunately she was most dissatisfied at what had happened to her, and looked positively owlish in displeasure, not to say terrifying. I overcame my terror in this dream because of my desire to help her, that is, encourage her to accept the inevitable and fly out into the freedom of the great blue Beyond. So the angry dead by degrees are appeased. - Tomorrow we escape this blustering winter weather for a holiday on Madeira.

Funchal. The same hotel as always, the view from our room as always, the Atlantic ... Fish and wine and waves! The little restaurant, almost a shack, on a rock jutting out into the Atlantic. Clams and garlic, another bottle of wine, sea bass! All the restaurant windows are wide open. Below the sea rolls smoothly, every now and then an extra large wave, the reason why bathing in the sea on this island can be dangerous - an extra large wave rolls in, and we see it pour over the black rocks, see its pattern of flow and eddy, and a fine spray rises. My wife has the view of the sunset. I turn my chair to watch - what a display! As if life blood were spilling and splashing across the horizon.

8 April. The owl has flown to this island, I can hardly believe it. From the hotel balcony, gazing out to sea, this evening I saw a cruiser on the horizon, as it drew near I scanned it with my binoculars and picked out a word: *EUROPA*. Of all the ports of this world, the points on the oceans, that at this moment as I stand on the balcony, this ship should be here, heading for Funchal!

9 April. So I see her again! With that so dangerous

charm I imagine her, from Funchal to Montevideo she sails with a smile of malice, with contempt for her travelling companions, the wealthy Germans; from Montevideo to Puerto Madryn, from Puerto Madryn to Ushuaia her anxiety grows, bordering on confusion, and on through the Straits of Magellan with a dawning grief, but not yet prepared for the end. She only said goodbye in the last minutes of her life, after an afternoon of such vigorous snoring it seemed the end would never come. Then she waved her arms in the air and lifted her feet in their pink bed socks and shook them as if she were doing her exercises to restore her circulation. I called the nurse who told me I was seeing 'terminal restlessness'. My daughter and I watched by her bed, listened to her breathing. She opened her eyes, and in those clouded, perhaps blind eyes I read her goodbye. I leaned over her so that she could see me, if see me she could. Perhaps for twenty minutes I held her gaze, then her eyes closed.

After hungrily drawing in air her breathing stopped. It's happened, I thought. Without exhaling, she again breathed in deeply. Her chest rose. For a last time she was a giantess. Then the air fled.

She's died, I thought.

She inhaled again, deeply. We were crying, but we laughed. How like her! Then she died.

The sudden vivid memory of her head on the pillow after she had died plunged me into a depression that lifted when we then went to the Botanical Garden with its magnificent trees and orchids, its euphorbias and cacti.

24 April. Depression, but there's an excitement to it. A new life is surely beginning. I am on a new journey. Still, I

take refuge in the garden where I light fires in the incinerator, like a pyromaniac. Flames and smoke always cheer me.

25 April. I like to remember her, but clearing her flat disturbs. A terrible mother, I sometimes think. This perhaps won't be my final vision of her, but a starting point, a root ball . . . from which flowers will spring. I leant down to pick up a tennis racket in a cupboard where two of my mother's dresses still hang. Their hems brushed against my head, for a moment I felt my mother's presence, her touch, the warmth and comfort she had given me in my early years.

27 April. And so it goes on . . . a mild day, lush and green after rain, blossoms on the fruit trees, I'm remembering, remembering . . . what? Being a child, being filled with love is the memory this melancholy, beautiful, grey-green morning brings. Not sadness, but happiness: the gift of life, fullness, but fullness is a yearning for something, for someone, and at the same time a sense of the presence of that something, or someone: love.

3 June. The removals men took away her furniture. I watched them struggle with the sofa that had to go out through the window. It hung suspended from the third floor, the sun was shining - it was as if she, her life, were finally being moved, removed. Last night I dreamed sad dreams of bereavement in anticipation of today, though in my dream a little Jewish tailor said he would be doing a lot of mending for me for free... A sofa dangling from a building, sunshine, I was sorry I didn't have my camera. Handed the keys to the estate agent.

16 June. My mother's possessions, the Regency table and chairs, the Meissen plates and porcelain Cupids, even the painting *A Satyr Lusting after a Sleeping Nymph in a Landscape* are about to be scattered in auctions, her clothes given to charity shops. Their orbit in my memory will be a kind of primal *home*.

15 October. I am standing at the door of a vast room, my mother is in a bed far, far away. I wave but doubt she sees me. She is crying bitterly. Just then I feel a fresh wind blow into the room. She feels it too and this tells her she is still alive so her tears become tears of joy.

Will the past repeat itself? For a moment it seems as if the journey I made, now so many years ago, is still ahead of me. As if, once again, I'm in danger of some irredeemable loss ... Into the woods! That's how it goes in fairy tales, and of course it's true that danger is always here: seduction and enchantment. But we're not in a fairy tale, we're back in Bohemia.

We rise early and sit outdoors with steaming cups of coffee. The forest is dark and mysterious in the mist, soon the sun pours down its light. Soon the sky is a firm blue. My wife and I laze in the meadow, read and sunbathe, and cool off in the little pool, almost you'd think on days like this it was the Fountain of Youth. The heat keeps us like flies in amber. Eva leaves us to ourselves. She is a widow now, her Herr Doktor whom she married, has died. The sun at its zenith, bakes. The light strikes the rust-red trees that burst like fiery beams from the powerhouse of the earth.

I dreamed that dream again last night, the one I dream

often lately: the blue flower, the house buried under vegetation, not exactly the same dream, but an unravelling of the dream, a progress of the dream. The blue flower has gone, so has that jungle of vegetation beneath which so much lay hidden. What remains are the ruins of a house: this is memory, and I enter again and again, into ever new worlds of the past, into a kind of remembering that for me began on that first return to the house where I had lived in my earliest years. This remembering plagues me, wonderful and exhausting, it comes with the shock of waking, with the morning's light. A sentimental yearning, a dangerous undertow tugs me back to my father's grave, and to that nest of houses on the street that led to Nowhere, and to the entrance before which I shrink to a child's height, but where I am afraid to enter. Let that be a warning!

In September 1989 I had returned for the first time to my birthplace. By November of that same year the Berlin Wall had come down, in December the Prague regime surrendered and Communist rule came to an end in Czechoslovakia.

How warm, how sentimental our 'reunion' had been! We had drunk toasts: The family! The future! I had corresponded with Karel, but he had gone blind and the letters ceased. We sent each other Christmas greetings and condolences or congratulations, depending on the occasion. The Bernatrice farm was eventually restored to its heirs. Josef was one of these, had bought out the others, and now worked the farm. To the extent that I was 'one of the family', we had gone the way of many a family by more or less losing contact.

The map of Europe redrawn: the jubilation, the euphoria of 1989! Herz comes to mind, that moon face, the nicotine-stained teeth, and for a moment I seem to hear his voice, no less bitter and fierce now than it was then: It's the reconciliation that's criminal: forgetting.

Should we cut short our stay at Eva's and drive to Bernatice? Would a surprise visit forge a new link? In my mind's eye I see the interior of a house where I have never been, where my grandmother was born, where initials have been cut into a wardrobe that has not been used for firewood, where ancient rooms reveal their mystery. But no such house exists except in my imagination.

11/11/22 ✗

Printed in Great Britain
by Amazon